THE MILLION MOMENT

How Our Thoughts Shape Our Financial Destiny

MAC ATTRAM

Published 2019

THE
MILLIONAIRE
MOMENT

ISBN 978-1-9162493-0-1

Dedication

To my wife, Linda, and my three children T'yanna-Nicole, Destiny and Brandon for your ongoing support and understanding as I continue to follow my life's mission.

To my parents, Frederick and Eva, for imbuing me with my thirst for knowledge and understanding.

Acknowledgements

I'd like to thank the following people.

Steve Roche, my editor, for helping me to shape this book.

My team at MindSpace Associates for their commitment and dedication to training, coaching & supporting individuals in their pursuit of growth & more happiness.

'History tells us that success stories of all kinds start with a decision. Your financial success will start when you decide to read this life-changing book - **The Millionaire Moment**'.

T. Harv Eker, author of the #1 New York Times and International bestseller, Secrets Of The Millionaire Mind

"Whatever your financial life has been like so far it can change for the better, in a moment. **The Millionaire Moment** will show you how."

Bindar Dosanjh, award winning Author "Power Property Investing for Women" and Founder of "Female Property Alliance"

"Where are you now financially? In debt? In a dead-end job? Running a struggling business? No worries. Mac Attram has been there. In **The Millionaire Moment**, he shows you how to turn your life around and become a millionaire just like he did."

Peng Joon, author of Million Dollar Ads

Contents

The Millionaire Moment

It was 16 September 2004 and my life was at rock bottom. I was $100,000 in debt and running a struggling IT business. I was stressed, exhausted and hardly sleeping. I was working 80 to 90 hours a week because my business partners had disappeared on me. So I was working insane hours to ensure that the business had a chance of surviving. My wife was pregnant with our second child and, because of work, I wasn't seeing much of her or our first child.

On the morning of Thursday 16 September 2004, I took my daughter to an appointment with the doctor. The night before, my wife and I had fallen out over who was going to take her. I had said that I had too much to do at work that day but my wife was heavily pregnant. In the end, I agreed to take her. Once my daughter had been seen the doctor said that they hadn't seen me for a while and so they should just do a quick check-up. My blood pressure was so high that a look of concern came over the doctor's face. I was immediately booked in for blood tests.

I dropped my daughter back at school and drove off to work. On that journey, all I could think about was how high the blood pressure reading was. There was a history of blood pressure problems and heart attacks in my family. I didn't want to suffer the same fate. My mind was all over the place, as it had been for many months. But now even more so. I wasn't very attentive and had been picking up speeding fines regularly because I was rushing everywhere.

It was a normal stressful day of firefighting at work and I set off for home at about 7pm. On the way home, I'd often stop off at a particular PC World store to check out the competition. On this night, however, when I parked up in that store's car park I had no inclination to go into the store. Shaken up by the news that my health was in a bad way along with my relationships, my finances and my business, I just sat there alone with my thoughts. The truth is that I was on the verge of a breakdown.

I thought about the fact that I wasn't living the life I wanted to and I asked myself a couple of tough questions. The first one was: How did I create this situation? I realised that I had developed an ego. I thought I knew everything about business because I had been to university, had an MBA and lectured on business at The Open University. But what I knew was mere theory. I wasn't creating the results I wanted for my business because I didn't have the practical know-how.

Next, I asked myself the question: How do rich and successful people live their lives? At that point, I didn't have the answer to that key question.

The stress of the debts and my business failing was affecting my relationship with my family and my health. I knew that something had to change, and right there, I resolved that I was going to radically turn my finances around. I now refer to that decision as "my millionaire moment". I remember looking at the clock in my car at that moment. It was 7.55pm and it was the turning point in my life.

I threw myself into learning from people who had "been there and done it" in business. I did a home study course from Chet Homes and I put $1,500 on my credit card for flights and accommodation to attend a seminar called *Millionaire Mind* Intensive by T Harv Eker in Los Angeles. I resolved that, from that point forward, I was going to apply what I had already learned about wealth creation and what I was about to learn at the seminar.

I came back from LA and resolved to face and fix what needed fixing within my IT business. I sold the shop and moved the company to serviced offices. I focused on web design and stopped offering the IT support service. I had decided to lead a purpose-driven life and to follow my passions. IT had never been that for me so, once the business was in better financial shape, I exited that line of work.

I was fed up with working so hard and wanted a low maintenance wealth creation strategy. Previously I had tried stocks and shares and Internet marketing. I didn't like either and so decided upon property because I like to meet people and to help them.

I came across a strategy whereby I would find distressed properties that had motivated sellers. In other words, situations where the owners really needed to sell their properties quickly. For example, because they were struggling financially or because of a divorce or a death in the family. I fixed them up and rented them out.

The original plan was to buy one property a year for 10 years. It worked out so well that I ended up doing many more deals than that. All I was seeking at the beginning was financial freedom but, by 2007, to my surprise, I was officially a millionaire.

"To change your world you must first change you, you must change on the inside first. You must begin with yourself"

Mac Attram

Are you where I was in September 2004?

You know my story now, so where are you on your path? My guess is that things are at or near their worst for you financially. That's probably why you bought this book.

As bad as you may feel, however, what you may not realise is that you are actually in a good place. That's because it's when things are at their worst that you can get to meet your 'other self'. It's when you can come face-to-face with your full potential. Human beings are wired to be able to pull things out of the bag when the chips are down. We are wired for survival.

So whatever has happened to you to this point, you must never stop believing. It takes the same amount of effort to aim to become a millionaire as it does to stay where you are right now. Be open-minded to the possibility that anything can happen. You cannot believe if you have a closed mind. But when you have an open mind you can inspire faith, courage and belief in yourself and in others.

So make reading this book the turning point in your life and decide now to make this very moment your millionaire moment. Make a note of the current time and date of your millionaire moment. From this point onwards, there is a line in the sand and there is no going back.

In this book, I am going to share with you how you can become a millionaire. But what you're going to learn may surprise you. To this point, you have probably been looking outside of yourself for the answer. But the answer is in you and has been there all along. You're going to learn something that you have known deep down all along – it is that the key to wealth is how you think. When you successfully fight the battle in your head, then wealth will follow.

Let me explain. Did you know that the Chinese character for poverty is a symbol of a man standing at the bottom of a pit? He is bent over as if he is carrying a great burden. The Chinese character for money consists of three separate symbols. One means gold. The other two are spears. The first spear represents the outward struggle for survival. In other words, you've got to stand up, take action and be prepared to battle for money. The second spear symbolises the internal battle. So in other words, before you can fight the outward battle you must be willing to fight the battle in your head.

It's now time that you relieved yourself of the burden of not being wealthy. It's been weighing you down for too long. And it's time for you to fight the battle in your head. So let's start that process right now.

The first thing you need to do on this journey towards conquering your mind is to make sure that you are out-and-out committed to becoming a millionaire. Everyone likes the idea of becoming a millionaire but almost everyone hates the reality of doing what it takes to do it. There is a massive difference between wanting to become a millionaire and being totally committed. Wanting means doing whatever is convenient. Being out-and-out committed means doing whatever it takes.

So you now need to ask yourself a very serious question. Do you want or are you out-and-out committed to becoming a millionaire? If you want to become a millionaire, you may as well just stop reading right here and now because none of what I am about to reveal to you will make any difference. How do I know that? Because your desire is not strong enough to drive you onwards when times get tough. If you're out-and-out committed, however, carry on reading because you have the crucial first requirement to becoming wealthy – an intense desire.

So as you know, the path to becoming a millionaire starts with the Millionaire Moment.

The next steps are as follows.

- **Understanding the Natural Laws of the Universe when it comes to making money such as The Law of Abundance and The Law of Attraction.**

- **Understanding how the brain works and using that knowledge to think, feel and act differently.**

- **Changing your mindset by abandoning Poverty Thinking and taking up Wealthy Thinking.**

We will go through these four steps in this book. Plus afterwards, I will share some amazing rags to riches stories with you that will prove to you that anyone – including you – can do it. Finally, in the Appendix, I will provide you with all important information and resources that you will need on your path to wealth.

"Your beliefs serve as a filter through which you see the world"

Mac Attram

Being a Millionaire

A millionaire is someone who "has a net worth which is equal to or more than one million units of the currency in their particular country".

All told, at the end of 2017, there were just over 15 million US$ millionaires in the world. The United States has the highest number with over 5 million. With 357,200, London is the city with the highest number of millionaires.

Other interesting facts about millionaires:

- 16% of millionaires inherited their fortunes.

- 47% of millionaires are business owners.

- The average age is 61.

- The average amount a millionaire owns in assets is US$3.05 million.

So let's talk about what it is like being a millionaire. Firstly, as a millionaire, it's not like you have a million sitting in your bank account. Unless you are a multi-millionaire, it makes no sense to keep cash in this way. Cash doesn't appreciate in value so most millionaires have their money in assets such as property which go up in value.

Typically, millionaires have their money in the form of possessions, stocks and bonds. They may even rent their home and lease their car and invest the money that would otherwise be tied up in other ways.

A key thing for millionaires is wanting to maintain that status. Often what they have is not enough for them and their focus is on not losing what they already have. Plus they are continually looking to find ways to grow their net worth.

Despite what you have been lead to believe, most millionaires don't rent private jets or stay at luxury hotels every time they travel. They could, but don't regard that as the best use of their money. Multi-millionaires sometimes live that kind of lifestyle but not all the time.

Many millionaires report that the best part is being able to help others. This may include being generous towards their family, friends and employees. They also appreciate the fact that their financial status means that they are able to help the good causes they feel a passion for.

The reality is that most millionaires still go to work and it's normally through choice. Very few don't work, and these are often the ones who have inherited or been given their fortunes. The majority of millionaires who have worked for it, continue to work because they want to make more money.

"You must develop a burning desire to be the best you can be at the things you love to do"

Mac Attram

MindSpace™
COACHING

Do you have any questions or pressing challenges at the moment? Book your FREE 30 Minute Success Session (Value $497) now at:

www.macattram.com/strategycall

Becoming Wealthy using the Natural Laws of the Universe

You'll remember from your school science lessons that there are certain laws which govern how the world works. The law of gravity is one such. Well, there are other Natural Laws that you almost certainly weren't taught at school but which are nonetheless true. These laws work when it comes to making money so you'll need to understand and work with them.

The Law of Vibration

This rule is all about how everything in this universe vibrates or moves. This includes objects, thoughts and emotions. In other words, everything that exists in the universe, whether it is visible or non-visible, is a form of energy at its basic level. The form that anything takes is determined by the frequency at which that energy vibrates.

The Law of Attraction

This is the law that brings to us the things and events which are in our lives. These things and events come to us through the power of attraction. What we attract is based on the energies which we put out with our thoughts, words, actions and feelings as per the next law.

The Law of Resonance

The Law of Attraction is the process that *makes results happen through attraction* but it is the Law of Resonance which is behind it and that determines precisely what is attracted to people.

To understand how this law works, it might help to get a bit technical. In science, resonance is where an object vibrates in sync with and as a result of the vibration of a neighbouring object. This tells us that everything in the universe is invisibly connected. Everything communicates to act as a whole and the way that everything is connected is through vibrations or resonance. The Law of Resonance is the law that makes sure that all energy continuously vibrates at a given frequency.

Like everything else in the universe, our thoughts and feelings are vibrations. The Law of Attraction takes those vibrations and works a bit like a magnet to bring things and events to us in physical form which match the energies we have been emitting.

The Law of Sowing and Reaping

Sometimes also known as the Law of Compensation, this law says that we are rewarded based on our efforts and actions. This is all about "what goes around comes around". We can never be compensated in the long term for more than we put in.

So the amount of money you have today is your compensation for what you have done in the past. So if you want to increase your compensation, then you must increase the value of your contribution.

An upshot of the Law of Sowing and Reaping is what is sometimes called the "Law of Overcompensation." This law says people who always make it a habit to put in more than they take out will achieve great success.

The Law of Exchange

This is the natural law of giving and receiving. It says that we should be paid when we offer something of value and we should be prepared to pay when we receive value.

This law also says that wealth needs to circulate. There has to be flow and there must be give and take. Look at what happens to water when it doesn't flow. It becomes stagnant.

The Law of Growth

This law ensures that something always grows. So creation is constant. The kind of growth that happens is determined by the kind and the quality of the seed which is planted.

The Law of Abundance

This is about the fact that there are unlimited resources available within the universe.

The Law of Polarity

This law says that everything exists on a range and has an opposite. For example, there is a left and a right, an up and a down. This law states that these opposites are simply different manifestations of the same thing.

Applying These Natural Laws to Making Money

The story of how money came to exist is proof of the importance of these natural laws. Money was needed so that the Law of Compensation and the Law of Sowing and Reaping could operate. Money needed to be invented so that people had a way of compensating each other for the exchange of value.

People paid each other through bartering before money in its current forms existed. They exchanged items of value such as livestock or produce for other items of equivalent value. So a farmer might have exchanged some eggs as payment to have his shoes repaired by the cobbler.

In larger towns and cities, however, it wasn't always convenient to transport livestock over longer distances so a more portable equivalent was required and this why coins came to be invented. The livestock roots still lived on, though, because some of the earliest coins carried an image of a cow's head. Interestingly, the word capital derives from the Latin word kaput, which means head. Most coins these days still have a head on one side and the other side is often called tails.

As commerce developed, coins themselves then became inefficient and too heavy to carry around in large numbers. Consequently, paper forms of money such as notes and cheques were created. As commerce developed even further and large amounts of money needed to be exchanged, letters of credit emerged.

As people began to travel more, a more secure format for money was required which is why the plastic card was invented. Now modern technology has brought a more convenient format in the shape of electronic money.

"If your ambitions are not greater than simply getting by in life, you'll never be truly happy"

Mac Attram

NOTES:

How The Human Brain Really Works

You have probably spent many hours and a ton of money over the years looking for the right *strategy* for becoming a millionaire. You have probably read about the lives of people who have become millionaires. You have probably looked for ways that you could copy how they achieved their success.

But while strategy is part of the answer, it's only a small part. Of course, you need the answer to the *how* question. But what is way more important is the *psychology*. Becoming a millionaire comes down to your thinking. Thoughts become things. So if your thinking is wrong then it doesn't matter about anything else.

The thing that you will use to become a millionaire is your brain. You use your brain to produce thoughts. Your thoughts become things. So working backwards, you need to change your thoughts in order to bring about the things that you want. And the way you change your thoughts is by changing the way you use your brain. It's as simple as that.

To become rich you will use your brain and the brains of others. It's going to be your tool. So you're going to need to learn how to use it properly. So far you haven't. It is the most amazing system in the known universe. Your brain is no different from anyone else's – it is as capable as the brain of any millionaire you can think of.

Most of the major discoveries which have been made about how the brain works have been made in the last 15 years. So unless you've been keeping pace with these findings, most of what you think you know about how your brain works is probably wrong. There are many myths that need to be exploded.

Your brain controls virtually everything you do. It uses 20% of the oxygen you breathe and 20% of the energy you use. The oxygen and energy are required to power the many thousands of chemical reactions that take place in your brain every second. These chemical reactions are behind your behaviours and your actions.

So let's start by understanding the human brain.

The Three Brains

Your brain is basically three brains in one. Each part is built on top of the other. Each brain performs different functions and has different purposes.

- The oldest part is the **Primitive Brain**, which is sometimes known as the **reptilian brain**.

- The next oldest part of the brain is the **Limbic Brain**, sometimes known as the **mammalian brain** or the emotional brain. Again this brain has a very powerful part to play in how you think.

- The third part is the **Neocortex** or **human brain**. It is responsible for advanced levels of thinking and skills such as analysis and speech.

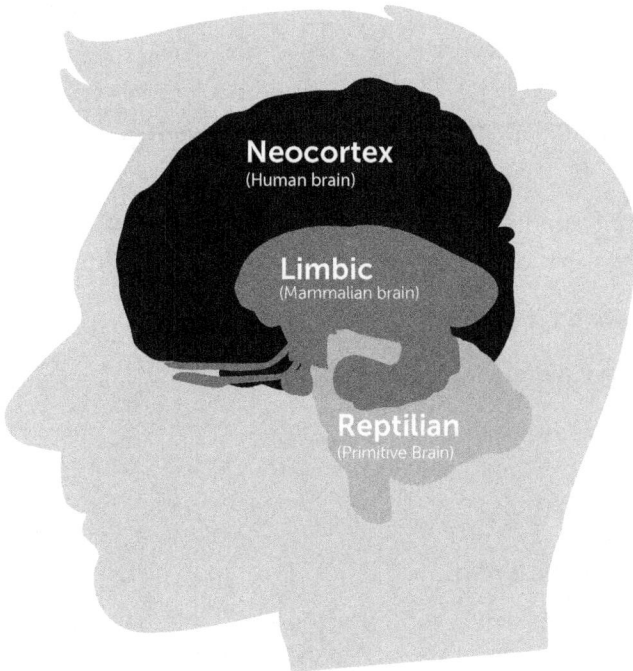

The Primitive Brain

The primitive brain connects the brain to the spinal column. It is similar to the entire brain of a reptile.

Although two new sections have been added to the brain, the primitive brain is still hugely influential. That's because its purposes include ensuring your survival and safety. It is responsible for what is known as the fight/flight/freeze response.

The biggest drive we have as humans is to survive. So when the primitive brain senses danger it takes over and overrides the other parts of your brain.

The primitive brain is responsible for determining your overall level of alertness and consciousness. It also controls important body processes such as breathing and your heartbeat. All the motor and sensory nerves go through the primitive brain on their way to the rest of the body.

There is a part of the primitive brain known as the Reticular Activating System. It is like a security guard or a gatekeeper. It screens all types of information that come in through your senses and decides what is allowed through to the higher functioning parts of your brain.

It filters out things that are regarded as irrelevant. The two types of information that are let through are information:

- **which is valuable to have right now**

- **that alerts you to threat or danger**

The primitive brain's first priority is survival. It is programmed to help you to avoid pain and danger. Its second priority is pleasure. It is programmed to help you to achieve comfort and well-being.

The Limbic Brain

Think of the limbic brain as the emotional brain. Just like the primitive brain, the limbic brain works in the background but has a huge impact on the way that you live. It links the primitive brain with the human brain.

Its purpose is to generate emotions. In conjunction with the primitive brain, it focuses on avoiding pain and seeking pleasure. It also generates our body language and gets us into action.

The limbic brain contains the fear system. It detects danger and it reacts. It causes us to behave in ways that increase our chances of survival. The part of the brain that is involved with this is called the amygdala. Information from the outside reaches the amygdala directly from the thalamus. The thalamus is the brains relay station meaning that it directs information to where it should go. It reaches the amygdala before it reaches the human brain's. This is important from a survival point of view because it means you can begin to respond to perceived dangers before you know precisely what the issues are.

The emotions which are generated in the limbic brain play a very important part in how we think and behave. They are what motivate us to take action.

The naturalist Charles Darwin believed that emotions are adaptations that allow both humans and animals to survive and reproduce. They motivate us to act quickly and to do things that will maximise our chances of success.

Emotions are e-motions. They motivate us to act. If we didn't feel emotions we probably wouldn't do very much. We wouldn't survive.

We feel emotions in our body. We tense up or we relax. So what we feel emotionally we also feel physically. Emotions can make us feel comfortable or uncomfortable. They are signals for us to do something urgently or to stay where we are.

Emotions are also internal signals. We can use our emotions to work out whether what we have decided to do is a good idea or not.

The Neocortex

This is the newest part of the brain from an evolutionary point of view. It is about 2.6 million years old. Think of it as the human brain as its capabilities are what make us different from other creatures in the animal kingdom.

The neocortex controls thinking skills, reasoning, language, social interactions, learning, remembering, deciding, creativity and dreams. The human brain consists of a right and left hemisphere and the frontal lobe. Sometimes the right hemisphere is associated with creativity and the left hemisphere is associated with logic abilities. The corpus callosum is a bundle of brain cells which connect these two hemispheres.

When the older parts of the brain are triggered, they completely override the dreams and goals of the neocortex. Fear and safety always override rational thought. You are hardwired that way.

How the Three Brains Interact With Each Other

In a sense, our mind is two separate teams. The primitive and limbic brains are one side and the human brain is on the other. Each has their own agenda and way of working.

The human brain thinks dispassionately and is rational. The primitive/limbic brains are emotional and act instinctively. Either of them can take control, but they can work together. One thing to bear in mind, though, is that the reptilian/emotional brains are faster and stronger than the human brain.

The Three Minds

You might be wondering what the difference is between the brain and the mind. Think of the mind as the part of you that does the thinking. Whereas the brain is where the different types of thinking take place. You can see the brain but you cannot see the mind.

There are three minds.

- Your Conscious Mind is the part of your thinking that you are aware of when you are fully awake.

- Your Subconscious Mind pretty much runs your life. Your automatic thoughts take place in your Subconscious Mind. Sometimes you will become aware of these thoughts. For example, when you have a hunch or intuition.

- The Superconscious Mind is the term for the minds beyond your own. It is also sometimes known as Infinite Intelligence or the Mind of God.

The Conscious Mind

This is the mind of your five senses. It enables you to experience the physical world. Most importantly, it is that aspect of your mind that is able to reason. It allows you to choose. It allows you to decide to take a new direction.

The Subconscious Mind

This is where most of your thinking takes place. It is where most of what you experience in life is processed and stored.

Your five senses receive and store 10 million items of information every second. Your Conscious Mind can only process 40 bits of information per second. Your Subconscious Mind processes everything else. Your Subconscious Mind processes information very quickly. For example, if it senses danger it will react in a fraction of a second.

Your Subconscious Mind influences how you feel, the decisions you make, and the way you behave. And all of this happens below the surface. All this happens without your conscious awareness.

Subconscious thinking is the term for your thinking activity which is below your level of awareness. Your Subconscious Mind is like a sleeping giant. It sleeps waiting to act on whatever desires you have. If you feed it with positive and crystal clear thoughts it can bring you all that you want in life.

Every thought that reaches your Subconscious Mind from any of your five senses is categorized and stored away. You can recall these thoughts from that filing system any time you need them in the future.

Your Subconscious Mind receives and files away all your thoughts no matter what they relate to. It does not discriminate. This means that you can plant any idea into it. It acts on your dominating desires. Your job is to reach and influence your Subconscious Mind. It works day and night.

Your Subconscious Mind functions whether you make any effort to influence it or not. Unless you take control, negative thoughts such as fear and poverty will be the stimuli to your Subconscious Mind.

It is influenced by thoughts which are mixed with feeling. Negative emotions inject themselves into your thoughts and are passed to your Subconscious Mind. Positive ones must be injected by you.

You must speak to your Subconscious Mind in the way it understands or it will ignore you. The language it understands best is messages mixed with emotion, faith and clarity.

The kind of positive emotions which influence the Subconscious Mind are desire, certainty, love, enthusiasm, and hope. Infuse your mind with positive emotions. The kind of negative emotions which influence your Subconscious Mind in a bad way are fear, hatred, revenge, greed, and anger.

Positive and negative emotions cannot occupy your mind at the same time. One or the other must dominate. Make sure it is positive ones.

This is where the law of habit comes in. Eventually, they will dominate your mind so completely that the negative ones cannot enter.

The Superconscious Mind

People who access the Superconscious Mind are geniuses. You can communicate with the minds of other people and you can communicate with a higher intelligence. The idea that will propel you to riches will come from the Superconscious Mind. The way in which you will receive the idea is via your sixth sense. We think that we only have five senses but we don't. We can sense thoughts as well.

Neural Maps

There is a common misconception that the brain processes information in the same way that a computer does. Unlike a computer, it doesn't store or process information as individual items of data. It organizes data into patterns or neural maps as they are called. It forms thoughts from these maps as well.

Neural maps are entire chunks of knowledge, perception or thoughts. The brain perceives things through these maps. It relates one whole map to another whole map.

Another way of thinking about this is that the brain organizes its data into structures of preconceived ideas, patterns of thoughts. This is useful in one way. This is because it allows the brain to get through life without having to do lots of processing. So, for example, every time it sees a car it doesn't have to figure out what a car is. It goes to its neural map for cars where it finds all its existing knowledge, experiences, perceptions and thoughts about cars. The brain uses its existing knowledge as the basis for understanding what it encounters in the future.

So if you have a particular belief about something it will be stored in a neural map. That neural map will contain things such as your feelings, associations, memories and experiences with regard to that belief. Any 'evidence' you may have gathered over the years to support that belief will also be contained within that neural map.

Neural maps help the brain to make sense of new information. What the brain does is to link the new information to an existing map. There is a positive and a negative consequence of this.

The negative side is that our brains are far more likely to notice things that fit into one of our current maps. This can mean that we are not very good at taking on new information. This is why we generalise and stereotype. Beliefs and habits can become hardened. The default setting for the brain is to stick with what it knows. It uses less energy by doing this and it gets a sense of certainty.

NOTES:

"How you talk to yourself – in other words, the specific words you use – control the way you think"

Mac Attram

Poverty Thinking

Now we know how the brain works. We know about our survival instinct, thoughts and feelings. We know that our thinking is the key to becoming a millionaire so we'll go through the ways in which you have gone wrong with your thinking.

Poverty Thinking Habit #1: You Haven't Wanted To Be a Millionaire Badly Enough

Face up to the cold hard facts of where you are now. Whether you are willing to accept the following statement or not, it is true. It is true because right now you are not a millionaire.

Here is the statement. Right now, you have:

- exactly the amount of money you want; and
- exactly the amount of money you believe you are capable of having.

Be honest. Until this point in your life, you have *wished* that you were a millionaire. Being a millionaire has not been the most important thing in your life.

> *"When you want to succeed as bad as you want to breathe, then you'll be successful."* Eric Thomas

Also, you haven't believed you could be a millionaire and you haven't been completely clear in your thinking. You haven't set being a millionaire as a *precise goal*. All of these things are facts. Stop deluding yourself. You have got to be completely honest. You must see the situation as it is.

The fact that you are not currently a millionaire is not because you have been unlucky, or because you didn't have the right start in life or because you haven't had the right education.

Human beings are hardwired to do whatever is easiest. We are hardwired to do things which require the least amount of effort so that we can save our energy. This is part of our survival instinct. So you have got to override that human tendency within you. You have to do whatever it takes to become a millionaire and not what is convenient.

Poverty Thinking Habit #2: You Haven't Left Your Comfort Zone

You are too comfortable. You might protest at that statement and say that you are not happy with where you are financially. The financial situation you are in is obviously not ideal. If it was, you would not have bought this book.

You have to be willing to give up feeling comfortable. You have to be willing to leave your comfort zone. Comfort zone means: "a settled method of working that requires little effort and yields only barely acceptable results."

> *"The important thing is this to be able at any moment to sacrifice what you are for what you will become."* Eric Thomas

But giving up some of what you have in order to be a millionaire might scare you a bit. It's the unknown. Change is scary. It's risky. But unless you're prepared to give up what you are for what you want, you will stay exactly where you are. The bottom line is that you are scared.

Fear is nothing more than a state of mind. It is not real. Fear is an emotion and it is powerful. But it can be controlled. Understand that we are hardwired to fear things which threaten our survival that can take things away from us that give us pleasure.

There are six main fears. The first is poverty and the second is criticism. Our other main fears are ill-health, lost love, old-age, and death.

Your fears are buried deep in your Subconscious Mind. You may not be consciously aware of them but they are there nonetheless. They control what you think and what you do. Notice your behaviours, however, and you will get a better idea as to whether or not you have certain fears.

The chances are very high that right now you fear criticism from other people more than you want success. The fear of criticism is a very subtle fear. It can be difficult to spot. Some people fear criticism so much that they do not live their own lives. They fear any criticism that might come their way if they fail or if other people will not approve of what they're doing.

Most people allow others to influence them to such an extent that they cannot live their own lives because they fear criticism. So their fear of criticism is stronger than their desire for success. They don't want to be seen as crazy for setting big goals.

Any of the following traits or behaviours could be a signal that you have a fear of criticism:

- being self-conscious
- being nervous
- being timid
- feeling inferior to others
- copying others
- boasting
- showing off
- not displaying personal initiative
- lacking self-confidence
- poor posture
- having a bad memory
- dithering
- overspending
- lacking ambition
- gossiping
- criticising others

"At some point in life, you have to face your fears."

Eric Thomas

Remember that your fears lie buried deep in your Subconscious Mind. So often you do not realize you have them. But they are there and they affect you all of the time.

Poverty Thinking Habit #3: Your Thinking Is Infected With Viruses

You have the ability to become a millionaire but here are two problems.

- When it comes to money, our brains are preset at birth towards poverty and not riches. But you have never been taught how to replace your 'poverty setting' with a 'millionaire setting'.

- To make matters worse, you have developed habits and beliefs as you have gone through life which are negative. Some of your automatic behaviours are constructive, of course. But it's the ones which are unhelpful that have got in your way. Those bugs are a bit like computer viruses. They have crept into your Subconscious Mind without you realising. And once there, they have been working in the background and have been destructive.

The good news is that your brain can be reset from a 'poverty setting' to a 'millionaire setting'. And the bugs can be removed.

Bear in mind this crucially important point – your education or background has absolutely nothing to do with your ability to become a millionaire. To repeat – we all have the same hardware. No person's brain is better than anyone else's.

Fixing these issues is done by getting your Conscious Mind to communicate to your Subconscious Mind in the correct way. Your Subconscious Mind is extraordinary. It acts on the instructions that you send it from your Conscious Mind. It then works out plans and gives you what you want.

So what you have right now in your life is what you have told your Subconscious Mind you want. "But I want to be a millionaire," you might protest. Maybe so. But you have not communicated that particular message to your Subconscious Mind in the way that it understands.

There is a particular way of communicating with the Subconscious Mind. The things that you now have in your life are the things that you have communicated to your Subconscious Mind in the way it understands. It gives you exactly what you want and exactly what you believe you can achieve. That is a fact. So what you have now in your life is what you have wanted. Not what you say you want. But what your Subconscious Mind has understood and believed that you want.

So if you want to become a millionaire, you need to communicate that message to your Subconscious Mind in the way that it understands.

We all have the same brain but it's just that each of us has a brain which is programmed differently. But it can be reprogrammed.

Becoming a millionaire is about using your brain and the brains of others in the right way. And we all have a brain capable of great things. You just need to retrain it.

If you say that you believe you can achieve something using your conscious thinking and you do not believe the same thing subconsciously, then your brain is mixed up. Your internal image must match up with your external image.

Change happens from the inside out. When your subconscious self-image doesn't match up with how you think of yourself consciously, you will eventually sabotage yourself.

Don't think for one minute that you cannot change. One of the biggest discoveries in the field of neuroscience in the last few years is what is known as neural plasticity. We used to think that the brain is physiologically fixed. We now know that the brain can change. Neural plasticity means that the brain can and does change throughout life.

Poverty Thinking Habit #4: Your Financial Setpoint Is Set Too Low

The world responds to your thoughts. Thinking comes before results. So to get different results you need to change the way you are thinking.

As T. Harv Eker describes in his book *'Secrets Of The Millionaire Mind'*; a thermostat is a control mechanism which senses the temperature of a system. It is set to a desired temperature and its purpose is to keep the temperature near or at that setpoint. It does this by switching the heating on or cooling it down.

He says, similarly, you have a money thermostat inside your brain. It is part of your self-image. Whatever you subconsciously believe about yourself from a financial point of view will be reflected in your financial thermostat setting. So as you go through life the reality of your financial situation will remain at or near your setpoint.

If you do come into a lot of money your financial thermostat will kick into action. The trick is to change the setpoint to a higher level. T. Harv Eker often gives the example of lottery winners. Look how many return to where they were financially within 3 to 5 years. Research estimates that 70 per cent of people who unexpectedly come into large sums of money lose it within seven years.

Poverty Thinking Habit #5: You Are Not Aware Of the Hidden Thoughts Which Are Running Your Life

It all comes down to what and how you think. What you probably don't realise is how unaware you are of most of what you think.

Right now, you are only aware of about 10% of your thoughts. These are the thoughts that occur in your Conscious Mind. You are unaware of about 90% your thoughts. These are the thoughts that occur in your Subconscious Mind. And it is these hidden thoughts which control most of what you do.

Your personality traits, motives, values, beliefs, habits, identity, and knowledge are stored in your Subconscious Mind. What is stored in your Subconscious Mind influences you way more than your conscious thoughts.

So you need to become aware of your hidden thoughts. And you need to change them if you are not getting what you want from life. There is a particular way of doing that which we will come to later in this book.

Poverty Thinking Habit #6: You Are Not Connecting Your Thinking to the Internet of Minds

Your brain is capable of communicating with the mind of any other person on the planet. Think of your mind as a computer. A computer which is connected to the Internet is way more powerful than a computer that isn't. You can do more with an Internet-connected computer. So it is with your brain. When you connect your brain to the 'Internet of Minds' you become a genius.

Poverty Thinking Habit #7: You Have Labelled Becoming a Millionaire As Painful

Even though the world is a far less dangerous place than it was for our primitive ancestors, our survival instinct is still powerful. Previously we faced the constant danger of being eaten alive. Nowadays that is obviously not the case.

But the primitive part of the brain is still programmed to steer us away from situations that the brain has labelled as potentially threatening, dangerous or painful. This is why we find it so difficult to leave our comfort zone.

Situations that we now find threatening can include a loss of control, not being approved of, walking into a room full of strangers, losing money and speaking in public. Of course, these situations are not really threatening in terms of injury or death. But bear in mind that the primitive and emotional parts of your brain are at work here. They are not logical or analytical. Their responses are instinctive and automatic.

It is possible that when it comes to the issue of becoming a millionaire that your primitive and emotional brains have labelled what that involves as threatening or dangerous. Perhaps they fear you will lose everything you already have. Perhaps you are comfortable where you are and get a certain degree of pleasure out of your current situation. If that's the case your brain is wired to avoid is taking the actions that will lead to you becoming a millionaire. So although consciously you may say you want to be a millionaire, the powerful, instinctive and automatic responses of the primitive and emotional parts of the brain may be working in the opposite direction.

"Thoughts are things. Every thought you have – be it good or bad – is a form of energy that can affect those around you."
Mac Attram

NOTES:

Wealthy Thinking

So now you know:

- why what you have been doing hasn't worked; and
- how your brain and your mind work.

So now it's time to tell you what to do. Your job is to reprogram the way you think. You need to change the way you think at a Conscious and a Subconscious level.

There are seven new thinking habits that you need to adopt. Plus you have got to communicate to your Subconscious Mind in a way that it understands so that it is reprogrammed as well. You need to speak in its language. This will mean that your goal of becoming a millionaire will become embedded at a deep level in your brain.

"Putting emotion behind your goals is crucially important. The stronger the emotion behind a thought, the faster the results will be achieved. This means being clear on why you want to achieve the goal."

Mac Attram

Wealthy Thinking Habit #1: Emotion

Everything that we create or acquire begins in the form of a desire. You need to want to become a millionaire more than anything else in the world. You must feel very emotional when you think about becoming a millionaire. You need to have an insatiable hunger and a white-hot desire.

Why? Because your Subconscious Mind takes notice of the things that you feel emotionally strongly about. Think of intense emotion as part of the language which the Subconscious Mind understands.

You will not get the results you are looking for unless you have hunger and desire. This applies to any goal and not just your desire to become a millionaire.

When you first come up with an idea of what you want, your wish is weak and brittle. Your wishes are like iron. When you add carbon to iron you get steel. And when you add fire to your wishes, you get desires. Think about the process for making steel. The carbon is added to iron in a furnace.

The way you intensify a desire is to think about it a lot. You must focus on your desire. Focusing means fixing your attention on something. You must focus on the pleasure you'll get from being a millionaire and the pain you'll avoid by becoming a millionaire.

Do not be discouraged if you cannot control and direct emotion in this way the first time you try. You cannot cheat at this. To influence your Subconscious Mind you must be persistent. You have to pay the price if you want the results. And the way you pay the price is with effort and persistence.

You've got to create a white-hot desire. Concentrate on the desire until it becomes a burning obsession. A small amount of fire makes a small amount of heat. A large amount of fire generates a lot of heat.

Think of emotions as chemicals. Because that is what they really are. If you mix emotions in the right way, then you create a genius state of mind.

Try this exercise. Close your eyes. Focus your mind on the amount of money you are hungry to make. See the money in your mind's eye. Do this at least once each and every day.

Wealthy Thinking Habit #2: Certainty

You must have complete belief that you can achieve your goal. You need to develop absolute faith that you will become a millionaire.

This is another way in which the Subconscious Mind works. It takes instructions which are given to it by the Conscious Mind when it is in a state of absolute belief. The Subconscious Mind acts upon this as if it were a command.

The way you develop faith is to repeat a positive affirmation to yourself until you believe it to be true at a subconscious level. An affirmation is a positive phrase which you repeat to yourself which describe how you want to be. As you will learn, this is best done when you are in what is known as a hypnagogic state of mind.

What you are really doing here is playing a trick on your Subconscious Mind. You can make it believe you already have this money. It will accept this as a fact. It will then work on and give you a plan for acquiring the money you desire.

Whatever statement you repeat to yourself you end up believing. This is the case whether what you repeat to yourself is true or false. People who repeatedly tell themselves a lie end up believing that lie.

The origin of miracles is certainty. Faith is a catalyst. You get direct access to what is called the Superconscious Mind when you are certain you will achieve something. Certainty transforms thoughts. Thoughts that are combined with certainty vibrate at a higher frequency than ordinary thoughts. Thoughts which are mixed with positive emotions are like seeds planted in fertile ground.

It is natural to be sceptical. Human beings have been sceptical about new ideas since the beginning of time. Scepticism comes from the reptilian brain. You can override your scepticism by continuing to believe that this will work no matter what. Very soon you will have absolute faith in this process.

So you must believe this process will work. You must have faith. Repeat – you must have faith. This will work if you do it.

The key to all of this is getting your Subconscious Mind to work for you. It is the most powerful computer the world has ever seen or ever will see. It gives you what you ask it for.

You use your five senses to control the thoughts that reach your Subconscious Mind. Close your eyes and see, hear, feel, taste and touch what it will be like when you have achieved what you want financially. Your Subconscious Mind will then make it happen.

When this starts to work, money will come to you from sources that you never imagined existed.

So start right now believing that you already have the money you desire. Doing so demonstrates that you have the belief. Behind-the-scenes in your Subconscious Mind your imagination will be formulating your plan.

This is a very important next step – when you receive the plan, you must act on it. You will probably make an appearance to you in the form of inspiration. The plan will not come to you if you sit down and try and develop the plan using logic and reasoning. To repeat – when your Subconscious Mind gives you the plan, start immediately to work on the plan. When inspiration strikes you must act. Do not wait for the right time. Act when inspiration strikes.

Wealthy Thinking Habit #3: Clarity

Understand this: thoughts are things. They are powerful when they are crystal clear. Vagueness doesn't work. You must know precisely what you want. Your brain is like a heat-seeking missile. You must be crystal clear in knowing what you want.

Envision what you want all the time. Picture what you want in your mind as you go about your daily life.

You can think yourself into anything you want. But first of all, you must know what you want. Precisely what you want. But knowing what you want is a skill. Most people have no idea what they want.

What you need is intense hunger and not hope. Make what you want an obsession. Stake your entire future on your ability to get what you want. So why not cut away all sources of retreat? That's how you keep a burning desire to achieve.

Wishing doesn't work. That's what most people do. The word wish means 'to hope for something that cannot or probably will not happen'. And it doesn't. The state of mind you need to achieve is certainty. You need to have absolute faith that you will become a millionaire.

Certainty is one aspect of the way that you communicate effectively to your Subconscious Mind. Your desire to become a millionaire must become a burning obsession.

You have to be definite and you have to be certain. So, for example:

- **Decide on the exact amount of money you want to have. Do not be vague. It's no good saying: "I want lots of money." Your subconscious cannot understand that aim. Say: "I want to be a millionaire." Be precise. What is your definition of being a millionaire? Did you know there are two definitions? Which of these is your goal?**

- One definition of a millionaire is "a person who has a net worth that is equal to or exceeds one million units of their currency".

- The second is "a person who owns one million units of their currency in a bank account or savings account".

- **Decide on what you are prepared to do in order to become a millionaire.**

- **Decide the definite date by which you intend to be a millionaire.**

Turn this into a written statement. If you have a voice recorder or a smartphone with a voice recorder app, record the statement. Read your written statement out loud and listen to your recording at least five times a day.

You might feel that it's not possible for you to see yourself in your mind's eye as a millionaire before you actually become one. But you will have no problem doing this once you have a burning ambition to be the millionaire. Part of the answer is to intensify your hunger because then you'll have no problem already seeing yourself as a millionaire.

You must be definite. In other words, aiming to achieve your crystal clear goal must be a decision. The word decide means "to cut off all other possibilities". Imagine if you were to burn all bridges behind you. You'd have nowhere to retreat to. So you'd have no choice but to make it happen. That is a true decision.

Indecisiveness is one of the major causes of failure. You'll find that people who are influenced by the opinions of others do not make money. They allow other people to do their thinking for them. So they end up being hesitant.

Do not become tentative by being influenced by the opinions of other people. Opinions are cheap. They mean nothing. If you take notice of the opinions of others then you will be indecisive. Do not let other people do your thinking for you. You will have no passion or ambitions of your own if you allow yourself to be dragged down by negative people and what they think.

People who have an inferiority complex end up that way because they had their confidence taken away by other people voicing their opinions and ridiculing them.

You have a brain of your own. Use it. Believe that it is as capable as anyone else's. It most definitely is. You may not have used it properly to this point, but it does not mean that you cannot use it from now on to become a millionaire. Make up your own mind.

By all means, go to other people for facts and information. Use the Internet and books for this as well. Listen to the opinions of other people. But take them for what they are. They're not facts and they are not accurate predictions of what you will achieve in the future.

Seek out the opinions of wise people. Often they do not offer their opinions very much. Often they are modest. But when they do speak, you should listen intently.

You need to develop the ability to learn to form decisions from information, ideas and opinions. You then need to take action on those decisions. Decide quickly and firmly. That's what leaders do. A decisive mind has tremendous power.

You don't need to be ruthless to make lots of money. Rich people are wrongly considered to be that way. That is mistaken. What they are is decisive. When they make a decision that is it. In their mind, it is done. They do not back-track or make excuses.

The word "decision" comes from the Latin word "decisio", which means a cutting off. The verb is decidere, which means "to cut off".

So be decisive. When you make a decision, in your mind, cut off the possibility of not doing what you will say you will do.

"Until one is committed, there is hesitancy, the chance to draw back, always ineffectiveness. Concerning all acts of initiative (and creation), there is one elementary truth, the ignorance of which kills countless ideas and splendid plans: that the moment one definitely commits oneself, then providence moves too.

All sorts of things occur to help one that would never otherwise have occurred. A whole stream of events issues from the decision, raising in one's favour all manner of unforeseen incidents and meetings and material assistance, which no man could have dreamed would have come his way."

Whatever you can do or dream you can, begin it. Boldness has genius, power and magic in it. Begin it now." J. W. von Goethe

Wealthy Thinking Habit #4: Enact

Your Subconscious Mind doesn't know the difference between reality and non-reality. So if you act the part of being a millionaire, magic will happen. What you should do is to trick your Subconscious Mind. You should pretend that you already are a millionaire.

> *"We are what we repeatedly do. Excellence, then, is not an act, but a habit."* Aristotle

Do you think and act like a millionaire? Read what Aristotle said again. What he said all those centuries ago is so true. When you develop the habit of thinking and acting like a millionaire that is what you will become – remember that we are what we repeatedly do.

Neuroscientists are discovering what happens biochemically when you change your body language. When you adopt a 'power pose' your brain chemistry changes and you feel confident and powerful.

Neuroscientists have also discovered the existence of what are called mirror neurons in the brain. When you watch someone do something you automatically simulate the action in your own mind. This is done by the mirror neurons. So you can reproduce or mimic anything you see and experience the very same emotions that person is feeling.

> *"To keep your mind on a positive track, you need to make a conscious and ongoing effort to monitor your thoughts"* Mac Attram

Wealthy Thinking Habit #5: Positivity

Success is a state of mind. Failure is also a state of mind. Your state of mind is whatever your dominant thoughts are. You will receive the things which dominate your thoughts. Dominant thoughts are like a magnet. You will attract the abilities, the situations and the people which are in line with your dominating thoughts.

So you will fail if thoughts of failure dominate your thoughts. All you need to do is to develop a success state of mind if your life has been a failure so far.

Ignore negative people. Often people refuse to believe things they do not understand. You have the power to control your own thoughts.

Wealthy Thinking Habit #6: Gratitude

Be grateful for all that you have. Gratitude raises your vibration and connects you to the Superconscious Mind. You should be grateful for everything and not just the good things. But the truth is that all things have contributed to your advancement including the 'bad' things. Keep thinking about that as well as all the things you will receive in the future.

Wealthy Thinking Habit #7: Think Big

Successful people think big, not small. They do this in relation to all aspects of their lives. Thinking big is about thinking about problems and situations:

- from a far-reaching point of view;
- in a deeper way;
- from a wider perspective; and
- from other points of view.

If you can get to a point where it takes over your psychology, thinking big will drive you towards greater levels of achievement. This is because, when you think big, you naturally think more clearly and more creatively. Your imagination will be stretched and your potential will be opened up.

Resolve today that you are going to stop thinking small about your life and circumstances. This is because the secret to thinking big is to stop doing the things that cause you to think small. They are as follows:

- Negative thinking
- Looking for excuses
- Being doubtful and procrastinating
- Thinking short-term all the time
- Firefighting your way through life
- Over-analyzing situations
- Seeking perfection

Thinking big means operating with no fears and as if you have no limitations. It means going through life with the belief that life is working for you and will solve any problems for you and remove any obstacles that might get in your way.

These thinking habits constrict your ability to think big because they force you to think small and to think about insignificant events and circumstances in unproductive ways. This drains you of enthusiasm and creativity.

The brain gets excited by big ideas and large ambitions. Here are the thinking habits that cause you to think big about your life and your future.

- Believe you can succeed and you will – when you have a 'can do' attitude then the 'how to do it' shows up. Think success, not failure. The size of your success is determined by the size of your belief.

- Conquer your fears – action cures fear and builds confidence. Indecision and delays feed fear.

- Get help from others – success depends on the support of other people.

- Never give up – examine your setbacks and that will pave your way to success.

"The truth is whatever you can picture in your imagination you can accomplish."

Mac Attram

MindSpace™
COACHING

Do you have any questions or pressing challenges at the moment? Book your FREE 30 Minute Success Session (Value $497) now at:

www.macattram.com/strategycall

The Next Steps

Having set yourself on the road to becoming a millionaire by shifting from poverty to wealthy thinking, you're ready for the next steps.

Reprogram Your Subconscious Mind

You will remember that the Reticular Activating System within your primitive brain stands guard and screens information. It's an aspect of the Conscious Mind and decides what gets through. Plus you also learned that information is stored in your brain in the form of neural maps.

What all this means is that it can be difficult to change your sense of identity. Beliefs and habits can become hardened over time. But we also know that the brain has the ability to change – physically, functionally, and chemically – throughout life. This is known as brain plasticity.

The six other habits help towards reprogramming the subconscious mind, but the way to accelerate this process is to use affirmations and visualisation when the guards of your brain are down. This is a particular level of consciousness known as a hypnagogic state. A hypnogogic state is the state of mind you are in between being awake and being asleep. You feel drowsy but still awake. You can train yourself to get into this state of mind. This is something you will learn how to do later in this book.

What is interesting is that children spend a lot of time in this state of mind. It is interesting and no coincidence that the first six years of your life are very important when it comes to what you believe. In this state of mind, your Conscious Mind does very little discriminating. Things you learn in these early years are absorbed and stored as truths and beliefs in your Subconscious Mind. These early years are also when you form your sense of identity. If you were repeatedly told that you were stupid, for example, that will become imprinted in your mind. That belief can become erased, however.

That's when you were programmed initially. The good news is that you can learn to reprogram your thinking.

You may say that you want to be a millionaire. You might believe that you can do it, but if your goal and your sense of belief are not programmed into your subconscious mind, it's not going to happen. It doesn't matter how many ideas you have or how many strategies you have learned.

If your conscious mind thinks one thing and your subconscious mind thinks something else, that is known as a chaotic vibration. You are sending out mixed signals. It means that your hardware (your brain) is fine but your software (your thoughts) are corrupt.

So you need to reprogram your subconscious mind. The fastest and most effective way of doing that is to visualise and to affirm your beliefs while in what is known as a hypnagogic state of mind.

You also need to know what the idea is that will make you your fortune. Again the way to do that is to ask your subconscious mind to come up with the answer when you are in a hypnagogic state of mind.

Your conscious mind has two main functions. It can decide what to do. And it can take action for a short period of time in line with the goal that you set. But it is your subconscious mind which is the power centre. It is responsible for your habits and behaviours in the long term. So if it thinks your goals are something other than what you say they are consciously, eventually the actions you take will switch to ones that are in line with your subconscious goal.

But if there is coherence between what your conscious mind decides it wants and what your subconscious mind is programmed to believe that you want, then you will have coherence. This is the secret.

What you need, is to twice a day – ideally first thing in the morning and last thing at night – get yourself into a hypnagogic state. This is the drowsy state of mind you are in just before you go to sleep and just after you wake up. You feel drowsy and relaxed. You are not fully awake but you are aware of what is around you. It is a trance-like state of mind. Your guards are down so it is possible to communicate effectively directly with the subconscious mind.

Although you naturally are in this state of mind twice a day, it is possible to induce yourself into this state of mind as well. An effective way to do this is by way of a process called brainwave entrainment. When your brain is in a hypnagogic state it is running at a particular frequency. Brainwave entrainment involves listening to a sound which is pulsing at that frequency. The brain has a tendency to change its frequency to the frequency of an external stimulus. So by listening to a sound which is pulsing at the same frequency as the brain does in a hypnagogic state for about six or seven minutes, your brain will slip into a hypnagogic state of mind.

While in this state of mind you need to ask your subconscious mind to come up with your big idea.

Record the following statement on a voice recorder and

> **[Enter your target amount of money] will come into my possession between now and [enter target date]. The money will come to me in the capacity of a [enter your chosen field of work*] and from other sources. I will**

---

* If you don't yet know your chosen field of work, ask your subconscious mind to tell you – it knows.

provide the most effective service of which I am capable in return for this money. I am certain that I will have this money in my possession. I can experience having this money with all of my senses. The money will come to me in exchange for the value that I intend to provide in return for it. I am awaiting a plan by which to accumulate this money, and I will follow that plan when it is received.

You also need to use your conscious mind to create the vision of what your life will be like as a millionaire. Write a story which describes what a day in your life will be like as a millionaire. Describe the sights, sounds and feelings you will experience. Write down the new beliefs you will have as a millionaire and write down the new habits you will have. Write all of this down and then read this into a voice recorder.

What you should do is, when you are hypnagogic state of mind first thing in the morning and last thing at night, play the two recordings to yourself. You will be commanding your subconscious mind to give you your idea plus you will be imprinting your vision of your life as a millionaire and your new beliefs into your subconscious mind.

There is a best field of work that you should be in. Deep down you know what that is. You can become a leader and a money-maker in an amazingly short period of time if you tap into your unique brilliance.

Each of us is brilliant in a unique and special way. Each of us can do something that no one else can do as well as us. In other words, each of us has a niche that we can occupy.

Part of life is striving to discover what that is. Life does not hide that secret from us though. Instead, we simply do not see it. Unless that is, we look. Clues are left in our daily lives. But because so often we are simply focused on making a living, we do not see what is there.

The world is like a pyramid of people struggling with one another. You have no choice in the sense that you have to join a struggle. But you have a choice is as to where to fight. Don't fight your battle at the bottom of the pyramid doing the same thing as everyone else. It is too crowded. It is easier by finding your niche and fighting your battles near the top.

The best way to become a millionaire is through starting your own business. The largest proportion of millionaires made their money this way. Find your niche. You will have very little competition if you do.

Never think that there are no more opportunities left. Look for the needs of human beings. Open your eyes and listen to what they say. There are always needs that you can fill in a better way

Always be on the lookout for opportunity. Look at everything. Opportunity might be disguised. It might come in a form you do not expect. It might be disguised as a setback.

Inspiration

The next step is to wait for the idea or ideas which will make you a millionaire. The idea will be perfect. It will be perfect for you because it:

- **will be in the field of work that is best for you**

- **and will be a great business opportunity as it will meet demands that exist in the marketplace**

Ideas are the starting point of all fortunes. They are the product of your imagination. The strange thing about ideas is that first you give life to them, take action and then they take on a power of their own. They sweep aside all opposition. They have more power than the physical brains which gave birth to them. They have the power to live on even after the brain that gave birth to them has moved on.

Your particular idea will come via imagination. Think of your imagination as the factory of your mind. You can make anything and solve any problem with imagination. You can turn your goals into reality.

There are two types of imagination.

- *Personal Imagination* is where you come up with ideas and plans by creating new combinations from existing information, ideas and plans. Personal Imagination creates concepts and plans based on what is fed to it in the form of experience, education and observation. This is the ability most often used by the inventor.

- *Inspired Imagination* is where your mind has a direct connection with the Superconscious Mind. It is the method through which you receive hunches and flashes of inspiration. It is where all new ideas come from. It is where you can communicate with the Subconscious Minds of other people.

Inspired Imagination only works when the Conscious Mind is working at a very fast rate. So, for example, it works when the Conscious Mind is stimulated to work on something which it has a strong desire to achieve.

The more it is used, the more willing that inspired imagination is prepared to work for you. The more you use it, the sharper it gets. In this sense, it works just like any muscle or organ in your body.

Children possess and use inspired imagination. The capacity tends to become weaker as children become adults. But it only becomes weak because it is not being used. It does not die. The way you bring inspired imagination back to life is through stimulation.

It is possible that you have yet to experience inspired imagination. The ability to receive an idea or solve a problem through inspired imagination is an ability we all have. The people who do use this ability are geniuses. You can easily become a genius. All you have to do is to use inspired imagination.

It may seem hard for you to believe that there is a direct link between your mind, the minds of others and what we call the Superconscious Mind. Connecting with these other brains is an advanced form of thinking. Hunches can come from the Superconscious Mind.

Thinking using inspired imagination is way more powerful than ordinary thinking. It is like flying in a plane. You can see way more than when you're thinking at an ordinary, lower level. This is because your ability to think and your level of awareness are not limited to the things that occupy your mind when you are at the lower level. It is the necessities of life which occupy your mind at that lower level. Limitations are removed when you think at a high level. Your vision is not restricted by physical objects such as hills and valleys.

Learn to Use the Sixth Sense

The way that we receive an idea or a solution to a problem via inspired imagination is through our 'sixth sense'.

Inspired Imagination is what separates genius thinking from ordinary levels of thinking. The logical and reasoning thinking ability you have is useful but is limited. That's because it mainly works by using your experience, education, and observation. Not everything you gather through experience is accurate. Ideas you receive through your inspired imagination are much more reliable.

The best inventors use both their personal Imagination and inspired imagination. They start with personal imagination and move onto inspired imagination if that doesn't solve the problem.

This is how you do it:

- Use one of the mind stimulants to stimulate your mind to vibrate at a higher level. The positive stimulants which the mind responds to by vibrating at a higher level include love, a desire for sexual expression, an intense hunger for fame, power, or money, music, friendship, a mastermind group, mutual suffering and fear. The most effective method is the one mentioned earlier, namely hypnagogic programming. There are two negative mind stimulants and they are drugs and alcohol.

- Think about the unknown factors and create a perfect picture of the unknown factors.

- Hold that picture in your mind until it is taken over by the Subconscious Mind.

- Then relax and clear your mind of all thoughts.

- Wait for the idea to flash into your mind.

The human mind responds to stimulation. Your creative ability is set into action by emotions and not by logic and reasoning.

"Many people protest that they are 'not creative' but the truth is that the extent to which we are each creative is related to our self-concept in this area. So if you think you are creative, you are." Mac Attram

How this process works

The way in which you communicate with the Superconscious Mind is very similar to that through which the vibration of sound is communicated by radio.

- Radio sound cannot be communicated until it has changed into a higher vibration which the human ear cannot detect. So the radio sending station picks up the sound of the human voice and modifies it by stepping up the vibration millions of times.

- Then it is communicated through space.

- The radio receivers picking up the signal converts the energy into the original vibration so that it is recognised as sound.

It is the same with our brains and with thoughts. Every brain is able to pick up vibrations of thought which have been released by other brains.

- You stimulate your Subconscious Mind to receive thoughts from outside sources. As you know, hypnagogic programming is one way of doing this.

- Your thoughts vibrate at a higher level and so your Subconscious Mind then acts as a transmitting station. The Subconscious Mind translates your desires into terms which the Superconscious Mind can recognise.

- Your **Superconscious Mind** comes up with the answer you need and transmits it back to you.

- Your **sixth sense** picks up the idea, solution or plan. It brings it to the attention of your **Conscious Mind** in the form of a flash of inspiration or a hunch.

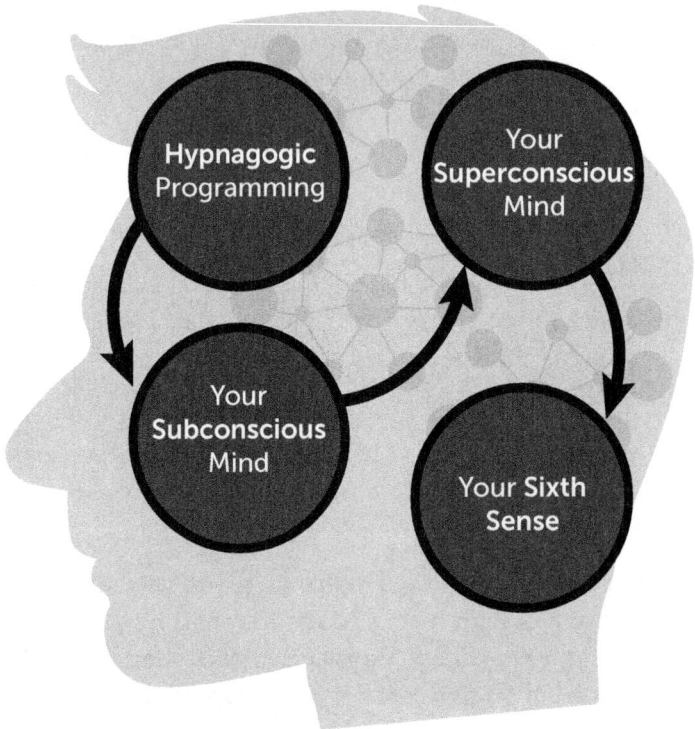

So understand that we are ruled by intangible forces. We have depended too much on our physical senses. We have limited our knowledge to physical things which we can see, hear, touch and so on. The other self is more powerful than the physical self.

Develop Your Expertise

Do not be put off if you do not have the knowledge or skills that you think you will need to succeed with an idea that you are presented with by the Superconscious Mind.

You can pick up any specialist knowledge or skill that you might need. This is especially true in this day and age. Either you can acquire the knowledge or skills yourself or you can find people who already have the knowledge and skills.

What to Do When Inspiration Strikes

Most ideas are stillborn. They have potential but they need a spark. They need to be injected with the breath of life.

And the way you do that is by creating specific plans and by acting on the plans straightaway.

A baby needs to be nursed when it is born. It is the same with an idea. An idea's chance of survival reduces for every minute that goes by after it's birth with no plans being developed or action being taken.

There is a reason why ideas are not developed and action is not taken after an idea is born. It is the fear of criticism. That is why most ideas are destroyed.

The importance of Planning

When inspiration strikes, you must write your plans down. This makes your thinking concrete. Hard work is necessary but is not enough. There is no point working hard if you do not know what you are trying to achieve and do not have solid practical plans. You need the power of clarity and definite plans as well.

If your first plan doesn't work, replace it with a new one. Keep doing this until you have a final plan which does work. Most people stop when their first plan doesn't work. Create new plans.

You cannot succeed at making money unless you have plans which are practical and workable.

Remember, that if the plan doesn't work it is simply a temporary defeat. It is not a permanent failure. All it means is that your plans were not sound. Do not be afraid to start all over again. If the plan doesn't work it just means there was something wrong with your plan. It doesn't mean that your goal is unachievable.

Remember that a quitter never wins and a winner never quits.

> *"One plus one doesn't equal two. It becomes the power of eleven."*
>
> Mark Victor Hansen, Author of the million-selling book, *Chicken Soup for the Soul*

Enlist the Help and Cooperation of Others

In order to turn your plans into practical plans, you need to borrow other people's brains. The best way of doing that is to form and use what is known as a mastermind group. This is absolutely essential.

Before forming your mastermind group, decide what advantages and benefits you can offer the other members of your group in return for their cooperation.

The Mastermind Principle is when a group of people come together in a spirit of cooperation and harmony to achieve goals, be they shared ones or individual ambitions. The idea is to coordinate the combined knowledge, creativity and effort contained within the group in order to achieve common and individual objectives.

A group of brains coordinated or connected in a spirit of harmony will provide more energy than a single brain. Just as a group of electric batteries will provide more energy than a single battery. People take on the nature and habits and the power of thought of those with whom they associate in a spirit of sympathy and harmony.

Whether utilised knowingly or not, almost all of the great accomplishments of history were achieved using this method. Since the beginning of time, probably, men and women have achieved great things when they've helped each other work towards definite objectives in a true spirit of harmony.

Examples include:

- Orville and Wilbur Wright working together to achieve what was considered the impossible by building the world's first aeroplane.

- Bill Gates and Paul Allen pooling their talents to create the most successful software company of all time, Microsoft.

- Andrew Carnegie pulling a team together that built the world's largest steel company.

- Also the writer Dale Carnegie, who wrote the famous book *How To Win Friends and Influence People*, attributed his success entirely to the Mastermind Principle.

For the Mastermind Principle to work absolute keys are for the people involved to:

- be positive, keen, cooperative
- want success for others and not just themselves
- work in a spirit of harmony

What happens when people cooperate and synchronise in this way is that they soak up and amplify each other's creative powers and result-achieving capabilities. When you blend mind power in this way, magic happens.

The human mind is a form of energy. When two or more minds 'mastermind', they form a great bank of energy, plus a third, invisible force which connects to the Infinite Intelligence of the Universe.

Take Efficient Action

Never take an action if you doubt the wisdom of doing it. Also never act if you have doubts or fears. Mistakes come from acting hastily. Go as fast as you can but don't hurry. Have faith.

You must always do all you can where you are. Do not think: "I am in a job I hate so I won't try."

This relates to a law of Nature which says that any creature will advance if has more to offer than can be expressed where it currently is.

Every day is either a successful day or a day of failure. It is the successful days which move you towards your goal. If every day is a success, you cannot fail to get rich.

You must do today the things that you must do today. Do not put things off even the things that may seem trivial. The consequences may be disastrous. This is because you do not know the workings of all the forces that may have been set moving on your behalf. The small things may be the very things which open the door of opportunity to great possibilities.

So do every day all that can be done that day. But do not overwork. And do not try to do the greatest possible number of things in the shortest possible time. Do not do tomorrow's work today. Do not try to do the week's work in a day. It is not the number of things you do but the efficiency of every separate action that matters.

Your actions will be strong and efficient if you hold the big picture of your vision in mind while you are doing them. Also, do them with faith and purpose. Picture the details of your vision in your leisure time.

Do all that you can do each day and make sure every act is efficient.

"The road to failure and despair is littered with the dreams of those who failed to act upon them – you must get into action." Mac Attram

Ignore the Opinions of Others

Ignore people who mock and criticise you. Everyone who succeeds in life in a major way is scorned. Typically they also get off to a bad start. You will have problems along the way. You will have struggles and seemingly impossible challenges that you have to meet. That's all part of the process. It's the same for every one who succeeds.

"Most of us never really reach the level of achievement of which we are capable because we don't challenge ourselves to do so." Mac Attram

Be Determined

You must be persistent. You must have an insatiable hunger, persistence and a burning desire.

Do not be put off when you come up against obstacles and have setbacks. If what you desire is extraordinary and not ordinary then you will not be put off. You will keep on going. You will not be discouraged.

It doesn't matter where you are in life right now. You have all you need. You are ready to start right now.

Persistence is a state of mind. A state of mind is your mood or mental state for a particular period of time. You are not born with grit. It can be developed and this is how you do it:

- **Make sure you know what you want. You must be specific and crystal clear. You cannot persist no matter what to achieve something if you do not know precisely what that is.**

- You must intensely desire what you want.

- You must be self-reliant. You must believe in your ability to follow it through.

- You must have plans. You cannot move forward if you do not know what the next step is.

You must have unwavering faith. You will have setbacks. Think of them as temporary defeats. Sometimes you may think that you have failed completely. Do not let this thought become what you believe. Do not quit. This is what most people do. Success is normally on the other side of failure.

You cannot succeed until you learn this lesson. The lesson is never to give up. Remember that success is often on the other side of failure.

Don't listen to the negative opinions of other people.

Whenever you fail, think of it in your mind as a temporary defeat. Do not be disheartened. The truth is that within every failure is a seed that could grow into something better. See failure as a signal that you should make greater efforts in the future.

You Must Value Yourself

Do you think that you deserve to be a millionaire? Every one of the millionaires I know feels absolutely certain that they deserve to be one. They feel like they have earned the right. The time has now arrived to stop telling yourself that you are not good enough or don't have the ability to become a millionaire.

My guess is that you have a very long list of excuses as to why you haven't already become a millionaire. My guess also is that you have a very short list of reasons why you deserve to be a millionaire.

You have got to value yourself. Remember what we said about the law of exchange? You've got to offer value and if you don't feel you can offer it then you have no chance of making big money.

"You don't attract what you want. You attract what you are." Wayne Dyer

You've got to put a millionaire valuation on yourself. Right now you have put a valuation on yourself called your financial blueprint. That valuation is whatever your net worth is right now. The financial results you have right now are a mirror of your internal financial blueprint. So to change your financial results you need to change your internal financial blueprint.

If you don't put a millionaire valuation on yourself, then the people and the opportunities needed for you to become a millionaire will not be attracted to you. You will repel rather than attract what you say that you want. You will repel the financial difference between where you are now and millionaire status. Interestingly, others will only value you in line with the secret valuation you have put on yourself.

You can imprint a new financial blueprint on your subconscious mind using visualisation techniques, affirmations or self-hypnosis. If you do this for between 1 and 3 months, you can gradually retrain your brain. You will start seeing and feeling the effects after a few weeks.

You can also change your financial blueprint by thinking, acting, and behaving like a millionaire. The exception to this is obviously to not start spending money on your credit card like a millionaire just yet!

"Fake it until you make it." Mary Kay Ash

At first, this may feel awkward. Don't worry as that is a totally normal feeling. When you do this your subconscious mind takes that message on. You begin to think, feel and act in line with the image that you are portraying. It's like being an actor. Your subconscious mind does not know the difference between reality and what you imagine. So the more that you consciously act out a role, the easier and quicker that this becomes your new blueprint. As you do this, you will no doubt get internal resistance from the little voice inside your head. Ignore it!

This works. Take the Hollywood actor Jim Carrey as an example. When he was starting out as a virtually penniless actor, he wrote himself a cheque for $10 million for acting services rendered and dated it Thanksgiving Day 1995. He put it in his wallet and kept it there over the years and sure enough just before Thanksgiving Day in 1995 he found out he was going to make $10 million for his role in the *Dumb and Dumber* movie!

So write yourself a cheque for the amount of money you want to be worth. Every time you look at that cheque you will be sending out an electrical message from your brain that matches your vision.

The Recipe for Making Money in Business

In business, the marketplace pays you in accordance with:

- the value you bring; and
- your ability to get people to exchange their money for the value you are offering.

Now to make a lot of money in business, hard work in itself is not enough. Other things matter such as timing and how many people you are serving. To make big money you need to be offering your products, services, knowledge or expertise to a large number of people or the right type of people.

As we learned with the Law of Compensation, you will get paid in direct proportion to the service and value you bring to the marketplace for which you charge for.

So here is the recipe for financial success.

Ingredients

- The Right Vibration
- Certainty
- Confidence
- Good Habits
- Enthusiasm
- Flexibility
- A Sense of Purpose
- Out-And-Out Commitment

Instructions

1. Write down your financial goal with absolute clarity.

2. Come up with your product or service idea that you believe has the potential for you to achieve your financial goal.

3. Figure out the knowledge, skills and strategies you will need to acquire or hire.

4. Surround yourself with your team.

5. Take action on a daily basis and build momentum.

6. Adjust your thoughts and plans as often as needed until you have developed a system that works repeatedly.

7. Enjoy the journey.

"It's an old cliché but it's true: success is a journey and not a destination."
Mac Attram

Step 2 is the often the one that stumps people so here is some additional information on how to carry it out.

Put simply, your job is to figure out how to bring incredible products or services and more value to more people. If you do this, people will gladly hand over their money.

Sounds simple, and the good news is that there is a formula for doing this. Start by asking yourself this question: Based on my skills, knowledge and interests, what need in the marketplace shall I meet with a product or service idea?

When you have the answer, then your job is to make what you offer unique and better quality as compared to the similar products or services that are being offered in the marketplace. Specialist and Quality is better than General and Average.

Then you need to get very good at marketing and selling product or service. To earn big money in today's crowded marketplaces, you have to become a marketing and selling expert or hire, barter or partner with one. They are worth their weight in gold.

If you have an unremarkable product or service which is of average quality and added to which you have average-level marketing and selling skills, you will earn an average or just below average income. 95% of your competitors will also be average and data shows that across all industries the average companies will share no more than 20% of all the revenues for that product or service category. The remaining above-average competitors will earn the remaining four-fifths of the revenues.

Combining It All Together

Think of yourself as a chemist. You can combine chemicals in your brain to make a potent cocktail. The chemicals are called clarity, emotion, certainty and determination.

So you need:

- a clear and precise **vision** of you being a millionaire and a firm decision to go after it;

- an **intense hunger** to get what you want;

- the **certainty** that you will get what you want;

- a **positive state of mind** including a never-say-die attitude;

- the habit of thinking, feeling and **acting as if** you already are a millionaire;

- a sense of **gratitude** for what you already have and what you will have in the future; and

- to use **hypnagogic programming of your subconscious mind** to come up with the answers to your challenges, to affirm your beliefs and to visualise your vision.

This is a very powerful concoction. One of the most vital of all the ingredients in the cocktail is certainty. The Subconscious Mind picks up on certainty. It gets to work because you are telling it that something can definitely be achieved.

"Never quit.
Any obstacle can be overcome"
Mac Attram

MindSpace™
COACHING

Do you have any questions or pressing challenges at the moment? Book your FREE 30 Minute Success Session (Value $497) now at:

www.macattram.com/strategycall

8 Financial Vehicles for becoming a Millionaire

There are many ways of becoming a millionaire and making a fortune. The obvious and most-often used way is by *starting a business*. The advice I always offer budding entrepreneurs on this subject is to start with the end in mind. Too often, small business owners simply create a job for themselves through their business. It's possible to make good money along the way as you grow a business, but the big money will come if you sell it. So build your business with the exit in mind. Make sure it is scalable and systemized and so is not dependent on you so that it can continue to be successful when you've moved on.

Investing in the stock market can be a great way to make a lot of money but, be aware, that it does come with some risks. The trick is to do your research. Start by looking into the current trends which you can do by subscribing to stock trading magazines and blogs.

Many a fortune has been made from **real estate**. Although there are variations on the themes, there are essentially only two ways of making money from property. They are from an increase in the value of the property and from rental income collected from tenants.

Internet marketing can be very lucrative but it can take some to develop. But the good news is that it can be started on a part-time basis and with only a small investment. The idea is to test and, once you find a system that works, it becomes a question of repeating the same steps until you get the results. Internet marketing is a broad subject and consists of a combination of marketing strategies with the main ones being affiliate marketing, email marketing, social media marketing and pay per click advertising.

Mobile apps are, of course, the hot new way of making money. If you want to create the next Uber, the best way to come up with your new app idea is to do what the founders of it did – that is, find a specific problem that you yourself encounter and build a mobile app as a solution to it. Travis Kalanick and Garrett Camp had trouble hailing a cab in Paris and, from that, came the idea for Uber. Don't be discouraged if you find other apps addressing the same problem because you almost certainly will as it's a crowded marketplace. Instead, think of a different approach that solves the problem in a better way.

There are quite a few money making opportunities within the world of **social media**. A key one is promoting affiliate products. Start by looking at the Clickbank website where you will find thousands of great products that you can promote on social media. Another option is becoming an Amazon Associate. Another is to create and promote your own information products such as an ebook, an audio program or a video course. Services such as Gumroad and Sellfy make it possible to publish and sell your digital products.

Many a large fortune has been made over the years from creating and selling **software products**. Reasons why developing a software application is a good idea include the fact that it has a much higher perceived value than other product types. We're conditioned to spend more on software and, as a product, it's harder to copy. Finally, it takes longer to make than most other product types so it is harder for the competition to catch up.

You can make money from having a business idea, an invention or another type of creation such as music. You can make money with intellectual property, as it is known, without actually having to make anything yourself through licencing. When it comes to **Intellectual Property**, you can come up with your own idea and licence it. Or you can buy existing IP and sell it to a company that you know is looking for a solution in that area.

"Work in a spirit of harmony and collaboration."

Mac Attram

NOTES:

Rags to Riches Stories – they've done it and so can you

Anyone can become a millionaire regardless of their start or current situation in life. There are also many ways in which to do it. So here are some amazing and inspiring stories of people who went from rags to riches.

Frank Kern

Now widely considered to be one of the elite-level Internet marketing gurus in the world, Frank Kern started out in the field in 1999 by selling credit card machines online. Early in his life, he really struggled to find success. He worked hard as a salesperson but he hated what he was selling and didn't enjoy cold calling and facing rejection after rejection.

He was always searching for the answer with persistence though. Then one day he came across an ad for a course on Internet marketing. He read the ad countless times before taking a leap into the unknown and buying the course. It made an impact on him and so he quit selling credit card machines door-to-door.

Eager to get going in his new field, Frank started by sending unsolicited emails – it wasn't illegal back then – and he did OK. He then discovered some seminar recordings on the subject of selling via direct mail and then bought books about direct response advertising and copywriting. He was blown away with what he learned.

But it took six years of plugging away at it before he started to achieve success. He was running online ads selling training manuals and eventually got to a point where he was achieving sales of $100,000 a month. It was then that he decided to take another change of direction and decided to teach other people his methods. Soon he became known as an online marketing guru and now has over 100,000 clients. His list of raving fans includes Tony Robbins, the bestselling author and entrepreneur.

The two main messages he now teaches are the importance of positioning and something which he calls 'Behavioural Dynamic Response'. In other words:

- **get prospects to like you before you try to sell them something; and**

- **deliver automated marketing messages to your prospects based on their behaviour.**

Frank believes that a key to the success he has achieved was the realisation he had that when it comes to business success, the most important thing is not the product or the marketing – it's the market. In other words, it's the people that are going to be sold to. Frank now teaches that it's all very well having a passion for your product, but if that passion is not shared by other people it's going to be a difficult and uphill battle which will likely end in defeat.

One of Frank's other success mantras is that the amount of money you're going to make in any market is directly proportional to the amount of goodwill that you have in that market. He teaches that you should create that goodwill by providing value to others from the very beginning of your relationship with them. In other words, give them results in advance.

He has lived by the principle that if you whet someone's appetite for what you offer, that makes them hungrier. He has achieved success by making his actual marketing itself valuable to his prospects. He has used his marketing to demonstrate that he can help his customers by actually helping them through his marketing. When you do that, he says, they come to you. You don't have to chase them and you don't have to use hype.

Frank Kern has come a long way from the days when he was selling his *How to Train Your Parrot* e-book by sending out spam emails. And according to Frank, success comes from helping others first.

Sophia Amoruso

Founder of the Nasty Gal Empire, Sophia Amoruso has led a classic rags to riches life. In 2016, she was named one of the richest self-made women in the world by Forbes magazine but her early years were very different.

Her story includes being diagnosed with depression and ADHD in her adolescence, being an anarchist college dropout, being fired from a high-end shoe store and being unable to afford important medical treatment for a hernia because she was broke.

During the mid-2000s Sophia spent a lot of time on the social networking site, MySpace. She was an avid vintage shopper and was getting lots of friend requests from vintage sellers on eBay. It was then that the realisation came to her that, through eBay, the world could be her marketplace. Because she was a keen vintage shopper herself, she knew that she could find stuff to sell a lot cheaper than the existing sellers could.

So in 2006, aged 22, she bought the book *eBay Business for Dummies* and launched her own eBay store called Nasty Gal Vintage. Many of the vintage shops already on eBay had very bohemian names but she wanted to call her business in honour of her favourite album by the legendary singer Betty Davis. In retrospect, Sophia said that choosing the name she did meant that she ended up infusing her entire brand not only with her own spirit but with the spirit of Betty Davis as well.

Her business soon developed a devoted online following of young women on social media. By 2008 revenues were up to $223,000. Legend has it that in that same year she was suspended from eBay for promoting her own soon-to-launch e-commerce store,

NastyGal.com. By 2011, revenues had reached $28 million and the reported figure for 2012 was $100 million.

According to Sophia, an important reason why she was so successful with Nasty Gal was presentation and style advice. She had always known that Nasty Gal was about more than just selling stuff. The mission was to help girls to look good and to "feel awesome". As Amoruso herself once said: "Put it on the right girl, with the right hair and the right attitude, showing people how they could wear it – that was everything."

A lot of the growth came from social media and word of mouth. It started with MySpace and it wasn't long before Facebook replaced it as an important platform for NastyGal.com. Between 2011 and 2013, Nasty Gal's Facebook followers increased tenfold and the company developed an uncanny ability to turn page likes into sales. Crucially, the company also used its presence on social media as a means of understanding and connecting with a target market.

In 2017 Boohoo Group purchased Nasty Gal for $20 million and later that year Amoruso founded Girlboss Media.

Chris Gardner

If you've seen the 2006 movie *Pursuit of Happyness* starring Will Smith, then you'll be familiar with Chris Gardner. The film told the rags to riches story of how he made it on Wall Street. Today Chris is a multi-millionaire and was CEO of his own stock brokerage firm, Gardner Rich & Co until he sold his share in 2006 to found Christopher Gardner International Holdings. He is also a motivational speaker, author and a philanthropist.

Chris didn't have many positive male role models as a child. His father was living elsewhere when he was born and his stepfather was physically abusive to his mother and his sisters. He and his sisters were taken into foster care when he was 8 because their mother was convicted of trying to kill their stepfather by burning down the house while he was inside.

When he finished secondary schooling Gardner decided to enlist in the US Navy. After that, he took up a position at the University of California Medical Center and Veterans Administration Hospital in San Francisco. A pivotal moment in his life occurred when he met a stockbroker called Bob Bridges and, from that moment on, Gardner's future career path was decided. He dedicated his time to training as a stockbroker.

All was not going well generally, though, in his life as on one occasion he spent ten days in jail as punishment for being unable to pay $1,200 in parking tickets. Gardner returned home from jail to find that his wife and son had gone.

He worked hard to become a top trainee at Dean Witter Reynolds. He got to work early and stayed late making calls to prospective clients with his goal of 200 calls per day. His perseverance paid off when, in 1982, Gardner passed his exam and became a full employee of the firm. Eventually, Gardner was recruited by Bear Stearns & Company in San Francisco.

About four months after his wife Jackie disappeared with their son, she returned and gave him to Gardner to look after. He was only earning a small salary but he accepted sole custody of their child. The problem, however, was that the place where he lived did not allow children and that place was all he could afford. He was saving money to rent a house they could live in together but for a year he and his son were homeless. He put his son into daycare and they slept wherever they could find safety. After Gardner had found a home, he resumed contact with his wife and had a second child with her in 1985.

In 1987, Gardner established the brokerage firm, Gardner Rich & Co, in Chicago in an apartment with start-up capital of $10,000 and a single wooden desk that doubled as the family dinner table.

Nineteen years later Gardner sold his small stake in Gardner Rich in a multimillion-dollar deal.

Chris Gardner is now a major philanthropist who sponsors many charitable organizations, primarily the Cara Program and the Glide Memorial United Methodist Church in San Francisco, where he and his son received desperately needed shelter while he was homeless.

Richard Dennis

Known as "Prince of the Pit", the commodities trader Richard Dennis made $200 million in ten years after borrowing money from his family.

At the age of 17, Richard started out as an order runner on the trading floor of the Chicago Mercantile Exchange. A few years later, he began trading for his own account at the MidAmerica Commodity Exchange. To get around the rule requiring traders to be at least 21, he worked as his own runner and hired his father to trade in his place in the pit.

Dennis left trading to study. He earned a degree from DePaul University and was offered a graduate study place at Tulane University but changed his mind and returned to trading. It was then that he borrowed $1,600 from his family. It cost him $1,200 to get a seat at the MidAmerica Commodity Exchange which left him $400 in trading capital. In 1970, his trading increased this to $3,000 and in 1973 his capital was over $100,000.

He made a profit of $500,000 trading soybeans in 1974 and by the end of that year was a millionaire even though he was still in his mid-20s.

In contrast to the vast majority of floor traders, Dennis held positions for longer periods. His strategy was to see out short-term fluctuations and hold over the intermediate term. In the late 1970s, he bought a full membership at the more expensive Chicago Board of Trade and opened an office in order to trade more markets.

He believed that successful trading could be taught. He recruited and trained a group of men and women which he called the Turtles. Eventually, after the trial period ended, he gave the ones who had successfully traded the system accounts ranging from $250,000 to $2 million of his own money to manage. When his experiment ended five years later, his Turtles reportedly had earned an aggregate profit of $175 million.

Richard is now the president of the Dennis Trading Group Inc. and the vice-chairman of C&D Commodities. He is a supporter of Flex Your Rights, a non-profit organization that educates the public about their constitutional rights during police encounters.

Jan Koum

In February 2014, the Ukrainian American entrepreneur and computer programmer, Jan Koum, sold the business he founded just 3 years earlier to Facebook for US$19.3 billion. The company is WhatsApp, the mobile messaging app and in selling the business Jan entered the Forbes list of the 400 richest Americans at position 62 with an estimated personal worth of more than $7.5 billion.

Koum was born in Kiev and moved at the age of 16 with his mother and grandmother to California in 1992. A social support programme helped the family to get a small two-bedroom apartment. To begin with, Koum's mother worked as a babysitter while he worked as a cleaner at a grocery store. His mother died in 2000 after a long battle with cancer.

By the age of 18, Koum had become interested in programming. He enrolled at San Jose State University and at the same time worked at Ernst & Young as a security tester. He also joined a group of hackers called w00w00.

In 1997, Koum was hired by Yahoo! as an infrastructure engineer. Over the next nine years, Koum and his friend Brian Acton worked there together. In September 2007 they both left Yahoo! and took a year off travelling. Ironically, both applied to work at Facebook when they got back and were both rejected.

In January 2009, Koum bought an iPhone and realized there and then that the App Store was about to trigger the creation of a whole new industry. He visited his friend Alex Fishman and they talked for hours about Koum's idea for an app. Koum chose the name WhatsApp because it sounded like "what's up". A week later on his birthday, he incorporated WhatsApp Inc.

To begin with, WhatsApp wasn't very popular but that all changed when Apple added push notification ability to apps in June 2009. The app gained a large user base, and Koum convinced his friend Brian Acton to join the company. Koum granted Acton co-founder status after he managed to bring in $250,000 in seed funding.

In February 2014 Mark Zuckerberg from Facebook asked Koum to have dinner at his home and formally proposed Koum a deal to join the Facebook board. 10 days later Facebook announced that it was acquiring WhatsApp for US$19 billion.

In April 2018, Koum announced that he was leaving WhatsApp and stepping down from Facebook's board of directors due to disputes with the company. In so doing he forfeited Facebook stock worth almost $1 billion.

Sarah Robbins

To begin with, Sarah Robbins joined the network marketing company Rodan and Fields simply as a way to earn a bit of extra income. She was a kindergarten and first-grade teacher who was worried about losing her job at a time when the economy was struggling. He husband's landscape construction company was being affected by the state of the local economy.

The company decided that they wanted to bring their focus away from retail and to tap into the social economy. They chose a social selling model and decided to continue building their brand through network marketing.

Sarah began freelancing for Rodan and Fields on a part-time basis alongside her teaching career. She admits now that she was sceptical about her chances of success at first. She was a shy teacher at the time. The eureka moment for her came when she learned that the key to the network marketing business model is that it is all about ordinary people just being who they are and selling to their friends and acquaintances.

So she began sharing the products and the story of the business and, very soon, people began to join her. To her surprise, she surpassed her teacher's salary by the end of the school year and was able to retire from teaching. She then established simple systems for her team to be able to duplicate her success.

Before the age of 30, she was making a six-figure income a month from selling Rodan and Fields products. Sarah went on to become the first consultant to reach the Million Dollar Circle, the first member of the company's Hall of Fame and she remains the top-selling consultant.

Her husband was able to give up his business in order that they could work at the Rodan and Fields business together. They now help other independent consultants to achieve what they have done.

Oprah Winfrey

Worth more than $4billion and with an annual income of $200m, Oprah Winfrey's list of accomplishments is immense. They include presenting The Oprah Winfrey Show for 25 years, which is the highest-rated television show of all time in America. She also publishes her magazine and runs the O.W.N. television network.

She is the richest African American and the first and only black multi-billionaire in the USA. She is also a hugely important and generous philanthropist.

Oprah is undoubtedly one of the most powerful and influential women in the world. When she endorsed Barack Obama in the 2008 election, it is thought that she single-handedly brought more than a million votes to his campaign.

What Oprah has ultimately always been about is telling stories that affect the human spirit and doing so in a way that people could see themselves in the stories. Arguably, she also pioneered the open, emotional and empathic form of communication that is commonplace in the media and society nowadays.

Her current life is altogether very different from how it all began. She was born into poverty in rural Mississippi in 1954. Her mum was a teenage single mother who worked as a housemaid. Until the age of six, Oprah lived with her grandmother who was so poor that Oprah was sent to school wearing dresses made out of potato sacks. She was later sent to live with her father, Vernon Winfrey, a coal miner in Nashville.

She was raped at the age of nine by a cousin and was raped again later in her childhood by other family members. She became pregnant at 14 as a result of the sexual abuse, but her son was born prematurely and died shortly after being born.

She did well at school, particularly in speech and drama. She won a full scholarship to Tennessee State University. Just before leaving for college, aged 17, she won the Miss Black Tennessee beauty contest and was hired by a local radio station to read the news part-time. At the age of 19, she dropped out of her degree to be the youngest, and the first black, female news anchor at Nashville's WLAC-TV.

Her next job was as a news anchor at Baltimore's WJZ-TV. In 1978 she was moved from news to presenting a failing daytime chat programme called People Are Talking. Oprah had found her calling and in 1984, she relocated to Chicago to take over a morning chat show called AM Chicago. The name was soon changed to The Oprah Winfrey Show. It was syndicated nationally and quickly became the number one talk show in the US. The rest, as they say, is history.

Bindar Dosanjh

When Bindar's parents moved to the UK from India, neither of them had an education and they were not able to read or write. What they did know how to do, however, was to work hard and to strive to be the best that they could be. Those traits left a big impression on the young Bindar.

Growing up, life was hard and her family didn't have much money. Bindar had a strict Indian upbringing and she and her sisters were taught that their role in life was to be a good housewife and a mother. They were brought up in the knowledge that one day they were going to have an arranged marriage. Growing up they were not allowed to have an opinion and had to do what they were told. They couldn't talk to boys, couldn't cut their hair and were not allowed to drink alcohol.

Bindar married in 1986 and moved from Birmingham to London. She eventually got a job as a secretary for a conveyancing solicitor. She soon came to the conclusion that she could do a better job herself so she embarked on course of study in her spare time to become a legal executive. She then did another three years of study to become a fully qualified lawyer. After qualifying, Bindar went on to rise the ranks in a law firm reaching partner level. She later started and ran her own award-winning law firm.

It was in property where Bindar made her fortune, however. Her journey up the property ladder started in 1991 when she became an accidental landlady. Her arranged marriage had broken down and she was left with a 9-month old baby to look after and debts to pay. At the time she was earning just £7,500 a year and the interest rate on her £50,000 mortgage was 15%. The numbers didn't stack up so she had to rent out rooms in her own house. She herself moved into a bedroom with her young daughter.

As her next step, she decided that she needed to move closer to her daughter's school. However, she couldn't let go of the family home so Bindar decided to rent that out while she saved for a deposit to buy her second residential home.

Once she became a lawyer, she had more money but had very little time on her hands. She saw an advert in the newspaper with the headline "Become an armchair investor". She thought that was exactly what she needed. Unfortunately, what she ended up doing was giving her financial power away to an investment property company believing they knew more and they would take care of her needs. It didn't work out and she lost hundreds and thousands of pounds along with her self-esteem and her confidence.

She knew she had to move on, though. It took what happened to her and what she had learned for her to finally make the transition to becoming a professional and experienced property investor. She took control of her life and got herself financially educated. She went on to source and acquire property after property and learned a huge amount more in the process from her mistakes.

Today Bindar is a multi-award winning, property developer, mentor, trainer and lawyer. She has a portfolio worth several million pounds. As an international speaker, she now inspires thousands of women globally each year to take control of their financial destiny with her message "If I can do it, so can you."

"Everything that happens in the universe starts with a goal or an intention. Nothing would exist in physical reality were it not for intentions"

Mac Attram

MindSpace™
COACHING

Do you have any questions or pressing challenges at the moment? Book your FREE 30 Minute Success Session (Value $497) now at:

www.macattram.com/strategycall

Appendix – **Resources for Aspiring Millionaires**

Tax Planning

Simply put, tax planning is arranging your financial affairs in ways that postpone or avoid taxes. It's important for businesses and individuals but is not easy because tax rules are now more complicated than ever. So it's important to hire a tax planning expert.

The definition of tax planning is:

The activities taken to minimise tax liabilities to ensure all available allowances, deductions, exclusions and exemptions are working together in the most tax-efficient manner to reduce the total tax bill.

It involves:

- taking advantage of beneficial tax laws;

- increasing and accelerating tax deductions and tax credits; and

- making maximum use of all tax breaks available in your country.

What you shouldn't do is to change your financial actions just to avoid taxes. The best form of tax planning is to use strategies that permit you to do what you want while reducing tax bills along the way.

Tax planning and financial planning are connected. Financial planning is about implementing strategies that help you to reach your financial goals. Tax planning is closely linked because taxes are such a large expense item as you go through life. For truly financially successful people, taxes are often their single biggest expense.

It's amazing how many people fail to get the message about tax planning until they make a mistake that costs them a fortune in otherwise avoidable taxes. The trick is to plan financial transactions with taxes in mind.

There are different tax planning strategies. Here are areas where an advisor would be able to benefit a business and help it to save tax.

Capital gains tax

Planning in this area involves taking a number of factors into account such as what is being sold and who it is being sold to.

Corporate tax

Planning strategies include deferring income or profits, bringing forward costs and taking advantage of capital allowances.

Private individuals can retain their wealth through careful tax planning. Individual tax strategies relate to income tax, gifting children, gifting family members, property and pensions. When it comes to Inheritance Tax there are tax planning opportunities involving the family home such as gifting, downsizing, remortgaging and insurance options. It is also possible to use available strategies involving pension funds.

Asset Protection

Asset protection is a set of legal techniques for protecting the assets of individuals and business. A trust is a way of doing this. It is where one party, known as a trustor, gives another party, the trustee, the right to hold title to property or assets for the benefit of a third party, the beneficiary. They are an ancient concept that dates back to feudal times.

Trusts are highly versatile instruments that can protect assets and assign them to chosen people now or in the future. A trust is a separate legal entity so the money is generally safer than it would be if it were held by a person.

Trusts can be used for estate planning and for tax planning. In some cases, the tax consequences provided by using trusts are lower compared to other alternatives. Assets in a trust benefit from a step-up in basis, which can mean a substantial tax saving for the heirs who eventually inherit from the trust. Assets that are simply given away during the owner's lifetime typically do not.

Trusts are established:

- **to provide legal protection for the trustor's assets;**

- **to make sure those assets are distributed according to the wishes of the trustor;**

- **to save time, reduce paperwork and, in some cases, avoid or reduce inheritance or estate taxes.**

Although there are many different types of trusts, each fits into one or more of the following categories.

Living or Testamentary

A living trust is a written document in which an individual's assets are provided as a trust for the individual's use and benefit during his or her lifetime. The assets are transferred to his or her beneficiaries when they die. There is a successor trustee who is in charge of transferring the assets.

A testamentary trust, also known as a will trust, specifies how the assets of a person are to be designated after they die.

Revocable or Irrevocable

A revocable trust can be changed or terminated by the trustor during their lifetime. An irrevocable trust cannot be changed once it's established, or one that becomes irrevocable upon his or her death.

Living trusts can be either revocable or irrevocable. Testamentary trusts can only be irrevocable. An irrevocable trust is usually more desirable. The fact that it cannot be changed and contains assets that have been permanently moved out of the trustor's possession is what allows estate taxes to be minimized or avoided altogether.

Funded or Unfunded

A funded trust has assets put into it by the trustor during their lifetime. An unfunded trust consists only of the trust agreement with no funding. Unfunded trusts can become funded when the trustor dies.

Business Structures

Getting the right business structure for a business is important for many reasons, not least because the decision can impact its growth.

The names used for the various structures may vary from country to country but the principles are broadly the same – I have used the UK names in this book. There are essentially four options and they are:

- sole trader;
- partnership;
- limited liability company; and
- limited liability partnership.

There are other options but you don't need to think in terms of these unless your intention is to raise a significant amount of finance. Let's look at the pros and cons of each structure. Operating as a *sole trader* is a good option for people who are thinking about staying small. It's often the choice made by one-person businesses who will probably stay that way or only ever employ a few people.

The advantages:

- You're in charge – you can make your own decisions and run the business the way you'd like.
- Everything you make is yours.
- It is an inexpensive and easy way of starting a business.
- There is very little red tape.

The disadvantages:

- In law, you and the business are regarded as the same legal entity. This means that liability is unlimited and so any business debt can be met from the owner's personal funds if the business fails.
- Can lack credibility in the market.
- If the business starts to grow, taxation becomes an issue because profits are taxed as income meaning that more tax can end up being paid.

A *partnership* is a good option if you want to provide services by teaming up with people you know well. Partnerships are a common extension of the sole trader model. A partnership is as flexible as the sole trader model.

An agreement needs to be reached as to how the liabilities, ownership and profits of the business are to be split between the partners. Partners also need to be clear on what happens if one partner wants to leave. In a standard partnership, all partners are also responsible for all the debts owed by the business.

Each partner's share of the profit will be taxed as income, as with the sole trader model. On the plus side, there is more potential to raise finance than there is with the sole trader structure but a negative is that a partnership can be messy to close down.

A *limited company* is a legal structure that, in the UK, is incorporated through Companies House and that provides limited personal liability to the owner(s) of the business.

Advantages

- Lends credibility to a business.
- Makes it easier to borrow money when the time comes.
- Limited liability if things go wrong – a limited company is a separate legal entity to the directors, so it is responsible in the event of difficulties arising.
- The tax regime is more favourable to a company than to a sole trader or partnership.

Disadvantages

- More administration as regards accounts and more red tape.

Limited liability partnerships are suited to professional services companies such as accountants and lawyers. They may be seen as a hybrid between limited liability companies and traditional partnerships. They offer the limited liability available to limited company shareholders combined with the tax regime and flexibility available to partnerships.

Saving & Investing

Saving and investing money is crucial. Creating a plan to save or invest is a way to manage spending habits and to prepare for future expenses. The difference between saving and investing is the amount of risk taken. Saving involves little or no risk whereas investing does, although the rewards can be greater.

The goal of saving is to preserve capital and to make a small return. The basic saving vehicles are as follows.

- **Savings accounts provide less access to your money than current or checking accounts. Financial institutions pay interest on the money held in the account, and that interest compounds over time.**

- **A money market account is a deposit account that's part current or checking account and part savings. The interest rate paid can be higher but there are restrictions on taking money out.**

- **A certificate deposit a deposit that is held for a specific term, such as three months, six months, one year, or even longer. During the term, the financial institution pays interest on the deposit. Each certificate deposit has different terms around how much is earned and when the money can be taken out.**

The definition of investing is "The act of committing money or capital to an endeavour with the expectation of obtaining an additional income or profit." The legendary investor Warren Buffett put it this way: "Investing is the process of laying out money now to receive more money in the future."

Another way to look at investing is working smarter and not harder. It's about making money work for you. It is also about making priorities for your money. Spending is easy and makes life fun in the moment but investing requires prioritizing our financial futures over our present desires.

There a variety of "investment vehicles" available and the following are the main ones.

- **Stocks investment where you buy shares of a company's stock and in so doing you own a piece of that company.**

- **A bond is a loan an investor makes to an organization in exchange for interest payments over a specified term plus repayment of the principal at the bond's maturity date.**

- Funds are where money is pooled from many investors and it is invested according to a specific investment strategy.

- Options are contracts that give the purchaser the right, but not the obligation, to buy or sell a security, such as a stock or exchange-traded fund, at a fixed price within a specific period of time.

Intellectual Property

Intellectual property is the term used to describe something which you create which is unique. It can be words, a design, a song, an invention and so on.

It's important to protect your creations to stop other people stealing or copying your intellectual property. There are various types of protection and they are copyright, patents, designs and trademarks. Some types of protection come automatically while others such as patents you have to apply for.

It's important to be aware that intellectual property can

- have more than one owner
- belong to people or businesses
- and be sold or transferred

Copyright relates to original works created by a person. The types of work protected by copyright includes books, novels, technical reports, manuals, paintings, sculptures, photographs, music, songs, dramatic works, films, television, and radio broadcasts, engineering, technical plans, promotional literature, advertising, computer software and databases. There must have been some skill, labour or judgment in the creation of the work. Copyright can be licensed or assigned to a third party. For example, the author of a book can assign it to the publisher.

A *patent* for an invention is granted by a government to an inventor and that gives them the right to stop others from making, using or selling the invention without their permission for a set period of time. Patents are territorial – for example if an inventor only has a UK patent they only have the rights in the UK and the rights to stop others from importing the patented products into the UK.

Trademarking relates to distinguishing the products or services of one business from another. Trademarks can come in many forms including words, straplines, logos, shapes, colours, sounds and even smells. When registering a trademark it is done within individual subjects, known as classes. This means that it is possible for other businesses to register identical or similar trademarks as long as it is in a different and unconnected class.

A registered design relates to the shape or ornamentation of a product. In other words, it relates to its appearance rather than to technical aspects or its construction. Registered designs have a maximum of 25 years of protection.

Financial Literacy

Financial literacy means to understand basic financial matters such as credit and debt management. With that understanding comes the knowledge and ability to make financially responsible decisions. This skill is so important because financial decision-making is getting more difficult for people because of the following trends.

- **Individuals are having to take on more financial decisions with less and less being done for them by governments and employers, with pensions being one example of this.**

- **Complicated options and too many choices – there are so many financial products on the market and they are more sophisticated than in the past.**

- **The ever-changing financial landscape means it can be difficult to keep up and follow a financial plan.**

A study conducted a few years ago found that people with high levels of financial literacy plan for retirement and have double the wealth of people who do not. It found that people with low financial literacy borrow more, have less wealth and end up paying unnecessary fees for financial products. They tend to buy on credit and are unable to pay their full balance each month and end up spending more in interest. They do not invest, have problems with debt and do not always understand the terms of their mortgages or loans.

Here are the basics of financial literacy.

- Creating and keeping to a budget is one of the most basic aspects of staying on top of finances. There are no excuses these days because there are a wide variety of technology tools available such as apps. Without having a budget, you can't hold yourself accountable and to know where your money is coming from or being spent.

- Understanding the impact of interest is crucial. Compound interest can really work in your favour as an investor or it can mean that you pay back much more than you need to if you are borrowing.

- Saving and investing have seemingly gone out of fashion, particularly with the younger generation. It's easy to ignore things like retirement, for example, when it seems so far off into the future.

- Understanding debt and credit ratings. Debt and credit can be extremely useful if managed correctly and a horrendous downward spiral if not.

"Visual clarity is power and that is the first benefit of picturing your goals."

Mac Attram

MindSpace™
COACHING

Do you have any questions or pressing challenges at the moment? Book your FREE 30 Minute Success Session (Value $497) now at:

www.macattram.com/strategycall

Resources

BOOKS

The Power of Masterminding
by Mac Attram

Would you like to discover how to apply the secret that great achievers such as Thomas Edison, Charles Wrigley and Bill Gates used to accomplish their success?

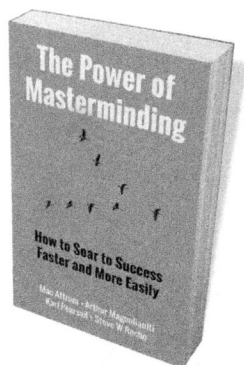

The key reasons that people do not achieve their goals are because they don't stay focused on what they want and fail to collaborate effectively.

You can't achieve major goals all on your own. You need to use the minds and resources of other people. The idea of self-made millionaires is a myth. Every great achiever, whether knowingly or not, has used an approach called Masterminding® to get results.

Masterminding® is an advanced form of thinking and teamwork. It's about plugging your brain into the minds of others and benefiting from their ideas, experience and abilities. It's about a group of people working in harmony with each other to achieve individual or group objectives.

In this book you will learn:

- how to form and run your very own success team
- the Masterminding® mindset, skillset and process
- how to accomplish your goals quickly and without stress or struggle

- how to draw on your Masterminding® team for a continual flow of ground-breaking ideas, energy, inspiration, feedback, contacts and resources, confidence, encouragement, challenge and accountability

Masterminding® will revolutionise the way you work with other people and achieve results.

The Inspired Warrior's Code by Mac Attram

This is not another self-help book that makes 'quick fix' promises.

In this book you will learn:

You will learn:

- a powerful set of success principles and techniques
- a proven, rich and powerful approach to living that will bring you all that you desire in life and more

Mac Attram is a former national martial arts champion. For him martial arts is not a sport but a 'way of living' aimed at achieving self-perfection through the union of mind, body and spirit.

As with martial arts, you will only understand The Inspired Warrior's Code when you practice it. But when you do you will:

- have the ability to create miracles in your life
- possess the courageous mindset of a champion
- be able to enjoy intense and absorbing relationships with all the people in your life.

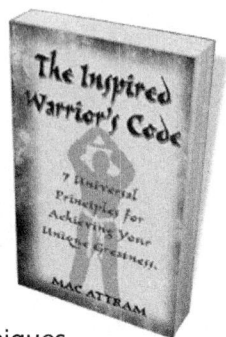

Face it & Fix it

*"**Face It & Fix It** is the shot in the arm that every owner of a struggling business needs."*

T. Harv Eker, #1 NYT & International Bestselling author of the book *Secrets of the Millionaire Mind*

Now a #1 International Bestseller! Half of all new businesses in the US and UK fail within five years. They fail for various reasons, but the main issue is that business owners either don't face up to their problems at all or when they do, it's too late. Running away from problems is a race that struggling businesses never win.

According to leading business growth expert and coach Mac Attram, it is always best to face problems when you are at your strongest and when your problems are at their weakest. That's where *Face It & Fix It* comes in.

Face It & Fix It is a must-read book for owners of struggling small businesses; those who don't have a moment to lose before disaster strikes and their business is lost.

Mac made many mistakes when he first started in business, as many entrepreneurs do. Things changed when he took his head out of the sand, faced up to reality and, in a systematic, ingenious and determined way, set about fixing the problems.

Face It & Fix It is a hard-hitting and easy-to-understand handbook that explains how any small business can be transformed into a success. Readers will learn:

- Why struggling small business owners need to finally face reality and the problems that must be solved.

- The 43 problems that research shows are guaranteed to lead to business failure if left unresolved. These all fit into one of the following categories: personal behavior,

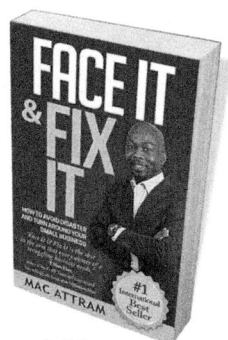

internal processes, external factors, or financial challenges.

- Seven inspiring, real-life business turnaround stories.

- The Fix-It Formula that Mac used to save his own business and that he now uses with his own clients as a turnaround consultant.

MindSpace™
COACHING

Visit **www.MindSpaceCoaching.com**
for more information

Services

Training Events

Mac Attram runs an exclusive selection of live training workshops, boot camps and webinars in the arena of wealth creation, business development and personal success for entrepreneurs and business owners each year.

All of Mac's live events are intensive, interactive and highly experiential, designed to bring you lasting improvement...

- Grow your sales rapidly using our proprietary method.

- Discover the secrets to success in life, business and money – from the leading business and personal growth expert.

- Gain clarity on the steps you must take to achieve your goals.

- Learn how to deal more effectively with negative & self limiting thoughts, so that fear, doubt, confusion or frustration no longer hold you back.

- Understand what shifts you need to make in your thinking – and how to actually make those shifts.

- Reprogram your mind to become more "success conscious" through exclusive solo, partner and group exercises – and make greater success your natural path.

And much more... including meeting and networking with likeminded people.

Mentoring & Coaching

Our 1-on-1 mentoring for entrepreneurs and business owners is designed to:

- Help you decide what goals and dreams are most important to you, so that you become laser-focused on the important things.
- Create a strategic plan to help you achieve those goals.
- Establish a realistic action plan so that you meet all important milestones.
- Implement an effective dashboard to track & measure all your key performance numbers, so that you know how you are doing at any given time of the month or year.
- Discover the "subconscious thoughts" that are holding you back, and then help you blast through them to achieve the life you want and deserve.
- All of these and much more will help you stay accountable, take action, solve business problems, and ultimately, progress faster and achieve

And much more... including meeting and networking with likeminded people.

Incubating

This is our ultimate partnering solution for supporting business owners who have an early stage business with high growth potential, who want to accelerate the growth and profitability of their business in both the short and the long term.

New business ideas are fragile and the chances of success can be increased with nurturing. With Incubating, we take an equity stake in your business and provide consistent, ongoing, 1-on-1 support to help nurture you and your business to grow stronger and faster.

Areas we can support you with include:

- Sales Performance
- Financial Performance
- Marketing
- Legal Context
- Team Building & Training
- Customer Service
- Strategic Planning
- Systems & Processes
- Operational Profits

Our goal is to help you build a business that can be run as a cashflow-generating asset that works with or without you – and which can later be sold or prepared for IPO.

Speaking

As a world-class trainer and keynote speaker, he knows how to engage, inspire and empower any audience. He has masterfully spoken at and facilitated large Seminars, Conferences, Exhibitions & Corporate Functions (nationally & internationally).

Masterminding

Masterminding is when a group of people come together in a spirit of cooperation and harmony to achieve goals, be they shared ones or individual ambitions.

The key idea is to coordinate the combined knowledge, creativity and effort contained within the group in order to achieve common and individual objectives.

There is nothing new about Masterminding. Whether utilized knowingly or not, almost all of the great accomplishments of history were achieved using this method.

Mac Attram is the author of the book, The Power of Masterminding, and is one of world's leading facilitators of the masterminding process.

A couple of times a year, he leads exclusive and invitation-only Masterminding events at beautiful locations around the world.

About the Author

Mac Attram is a multi-award winning speaker, investor, mentor, incubator, educator and author. In the world of business he is best known for helping entrepreneurs grow their businesses rapidly and for performing business turnarounds.

He has trained and coached over 100,000 people in more than 30 countries around the world in the areas of Wealth Creation, Business Development & Personal Growth.

He has shared the stage with some of the world's premier thought leaders and business experts, including Robert Kiyosaki, T. Harv Eker, Blair Singer, Lady Michelle Mone, Keith Cunningham, James Caan, Duncan Bannatyne and Les Brown.

Printed in Dunstable, United Kingdom